What New Zealand taught me about life and
the practice of medicine

BOX

OF

BIRDS

Stephen Stowers, M.D.

Table of Contents

Foreword

Like my great-grandfather, I became a doctor to help people. Along the way, I made some mistakes, as I'm sure most of my colleagues have, but my guiding light has always been to do what is in the best interests of the patient. Then corporatization swept through American medicine, clashing with my focus on the patient. This led me to move to New Zealand, and what I found there astonished me. I was not alone, for doctors I knew from around the globe who found refuge there alongside me learned the same lesson: New Zealand was a place where medicine was still focused on healing before all else, and we could feel like our best selves again. This book documents my journey from the system I knew from my time in the US (resource-rich, profit-oriented, and capitalistic) to the system I encountered in New Zealand (patient-oriented, resource-limited, with a socialized healthcare system). My colleagues who have read this work confirm it echoes their experiences too, and we have reminisced about our time together down under with real nostalgia, for only there were we able to practice with clearer consciences.

Chapter One

LOST DREAM

It was April of 2013, and I had just arrived at the hospital on the North Island of New Zealand. The fall nights were starting to get chilly, heralding the coming winter. In satellite images, New Zealand looks like two specks of emerald green in a sea of deep blue, a North and a South Island. The two landmasses sit in the Southern Hemisphere, just below Australia, and to my mind the seasons were juxtaposed with America's, as was the litigation-free healthcare system.

I was still acclimating to the changed calendar and the new medical environment. As a cardiologist with twenty-nine years of clinical experience in the United States, I had lost faith in American healthcare. I had almost lost faith in myself and in my colleagues, too. I had forgotten why I studied medicine in the first place, and what doctors could be. I thought I might find better circumstances in New Zealand and felt excited about that prospect, but also anxious about the challenges ahead. After all, I was "down under," eight thousand miles from home, driving on the wrong side of the road, and starting over in my chosen profession.

At the early morning hand-over meeting of consultants and registrars, I listened to a presentation about new patient admissions. Then I joined the cardiology team for morning rounds. One of our first patients was an elderly farmer with chest pain from a nearby community that has many cattle and sheep farms.

As I entered the open ward, I saw the patient, a white New Zealander in his mid-70s. He was lying on his back, and the golden morning sun filtered through the window, settling on his bare chest.

I advanced and pulled closed the privacy curtain. "Hi, I'm Dr. Stowers," I said. I began to take a history, while the team gathered around his bed. I asked what had brought him to the hospital.

He explained that while in the paddock herding his sheep, he had become "bad crook, bad crook, Doc," repeating the phrase as his bony hand grabbed at his hairy chest, which at the moment was covered with electrocardiogram (ECG) pads. The ECG pads were recording the electrical signals produced by his heart, checking for any irregularity in its rhythm. "Yesterday I was real bad crook!"

What does "bad crook" mean, I wondered?

He must have noticed my furrowed brow and the worried look on my face, because he blurted out with a smile, "No worries, Doc, this morning I'm a box of birds."

Befuddled, I looked to my Kiwi colleagues for assistance. I said, "From 'bad crook' to 'a box of birds?'"

Lia, a cardiology nurse with bright and cheerful blue eyes, stepped forward with a smile and said, "Yesterday he was feeling unwell and had chest pains. This morning he feels great, like a box of birds."

I was touched by the local farmer's reassuring words to his worried American cardiologist, but also frustrated at the unexpected challenge of not being able to communicate easily with the patient. I took out a small red notebook and started a list of Kiwi slang expressions that were used in the hospital setting. Eventually the list grew to include "ambo," short for ambulance, and the poetic though at first bewildering phrase, "He sucked the kumara." A root vegetable, the kumara is a form of sweet potato that was brought by the Māori to New Zealand when they arrived from Polynesia in the thirteenth century. To suck the kumara, you must be underground—in other words, you're dead.

These vivid colloquialisms soon became familiar to me, and I began to love the way that doctors, nurses, and patients expressed themselves. In the years since that moment, I have often been asked why I moved to New Zealand to practice medicine. Basically, I had become disillusioned by the physician's loss of control over patient care in the United States. During my lifetime, I witnessed an important philosophical shift in American medicine: the adoption of a corporate emphasis on productivity and profitability. The priority was no longer what was in the best interest of the patient, but rather what was in the best financial interest of the hospital system itself.

———————

For twenty-nine years, I had practiced in northeast Florida. I had been very happy in private practice, working out of (but not for) a hospital owned by the clinic. I was living the American dream of owning my own business, and I got to build close, lasting relationships with my patients. Then the bureaucratic shift in healthcare administration began. First, as a government policy, reimbursement for outpatient cardiac imaging services was cut, which made it harder to stay solvent in private practice. Second, larger hospital systems emerged that were focused on profits above patients. Third, I watched as my referring doctors' practices were bought out by competing hospital networks, and eventually I could no longer admit my own patients to the hospital myself. Instead, they had to be admitted by a hospitalist. Sometimes this resulted in poor communication, with patients being placed on the wrong medication, or even worse conundrums.

At this point, bevies of lawyers entered the scene. Malpractice lawsuits became another reason for my discontent. During my time in private practice, I had two patients die after what I considered to be necessary or advisable interventions. In one of those instances, a malpractice attorney contacted the family and brought a lawsuit against me and my colleagues that went all the way to a jury trial. This was an awful and distressing experience, even though we won the case after two years. Throughout the time that I owned my own practice, I saw commercials for medical malpractice attorneys flood the airwaves, asking whether patients had suffered from malfeasance at the hands of their doctors, and the amounts of money awarded to patients for pain and suffering skyrocketed. So did the cost to doctors for malpractice insurance, especially in areas like interventional cardiology, where every serious procedure poses the risk of major complications. By the end of my time in private practice, the cost of the Florida medical malpractice insurance coverage that I paid had risen to $60,000.00 US per year.

My overhead escalated, and it became inevitable that to continue in cardiology, I would have to sell my practice to a hospital. A new corporate hospital network had purchased our local hospital from the clinic in 2008, and once I became a corporate hospital employee in 2010, my dream of helping others swiftly turned into a nightmare. Once upon a time, local hospital administrators used to ask, "How can we help you deliver better care to your patients?" Corporate medicine asks instead, "How can we make you more productive?" The new hospital administration wanted me to generate more relative value units, known as RVUs in hospital-speak. An RVU is a unit of measurement intended to quantify each and every type of interaction a physician can have with a patient. An office visit might be 1.2 RVUs; a surgery, 20 RVUs. Today, most physicians' salaries are based on the number of RVUs they generate each day. I could spend an hour talking to a patient with a heart condition about the value of exercise, weight loss, a less stressful lifestyle, and cholesterol-lowering medication, and I would be assigned a low RVU and be reimbursed approximately $142 US. But if another doctor decided to take that same patient to the cath lab and insert a stent in the coronary artery—a quick 30-minute procedure—that doctor would be assigned a higher RVU and be reimbursed around $1,500 US. The hospital would also receive thousands of dollars for such a procedure.

Coronary artery bare-metal stents were introduced in the 1980s as a bail-out tool for balloon angioplasty procedures, tacking up the tear in the wall of the coronary artery that a balloon angioplasty typically produces. The stent repairs the torn flap of tissue, which could obstruct blood flow and damage the heart muscle if left alone. As coronary artery stents evolved, they were shown to be effective at saving lives by restoring blood flow during ST-segment elevation myocardial infarctions, or heart attacks caused by total blockages of the coronary artery, limiting damage to the heart by allowing oxygen-rich blood to flow to the oxygen-starved heart muscle. Stents have limitations, however, such as potential re-narrowing of the artery and clot formation within the stent, requiring prolonged administration of blood thinners. Stents also focus on one single point where there's an acute blockage, and if there is no restoration of blood flow to the rest of the heart and limitation of heart muscle damage, as there is when stenting a heart attack, there is no mortality reduction. This is because coronary artery disease is a diffuse condition, not a focal condition. Although it may look like there is a single point of narrowing, in reality, the entire length of the coronary artery contains inflammation and plaque that will eventually cause problems if left unaddressed. That is why stents don't prolong life or prevent heart attacks in stable cases of coronary artery disease, where blockages are present but not yet severe enough to cause an acute cardiac event. Coronary artery disease can thus be more effectively treated with cholesterol- and blood-pressure-lowering medication, risk-factor reduction, and a healthy lifestyle. Yet even though there is no evidence to show that stents lead to better patient outcomes in stable patients, they rapidly became ubiquitous.

At one point, an enthusiastic young hospital administrator in a three-piece suit met with me and showed me a horizontal bar graph of the hospital cardiologists, ranking us in terms of the number of stents we placed. I did not place stents in patients with stable coronary artery disease, because stable coronary artery disease can be treated more effectively with medication and lifestyle changes. Yet I was encouraged by the administrator to put in more stents so I could move up into the "top tier." The administrator was fresh out of business school, and the graph reminded me of a manufacturing report instead of a description of ideal patient care. It made me angry; in my view, he was all about generating profits. As I recall the conversation today, he never once mentioned how putting in more stents was going to improve patient care. The RVU system was heavily weighted toward doing in-hospital procedures, often without any proven benefit when compared with medication and risk-reduction through lifestyle. As if to emphasize this shift in priorities, the administration even changed the name of the hospital from the patron saint of doctors to that of the money-oriented corporation that had acquired the institution from the clinic. I became an outsider in my own profession.

I lasted one and a half years as a hospital-employed doctor, and my last day on the job was November 15, 2012. It was sad to me that the American dream of owning one's own business had faded, at least within the medical profession, and that the hospital had offered no safe harbor for a doctor who wanted to see patients thrive with minimal forms of intervention. I was hit with the shocking realization that I was almost a refugee within the medical profession, no longer the owner of my own practice and no longer in charge of my own life. I thought about trying to practice from a new berth at the University of Virginia, as my family owned a computer connector business nearby, but the potential opportunity turned out to be disappointing. The local community hospital would not let University of Virginia cardiologists admit patients to the hospital or use its cath lab—essentially kicking the UVA doctors out, so that the hospital-employed cardiologists could capture all of the revenue. Here, too, corporate America was sacrificing patient care on the altar of capitalism.

———

One day my wife Bonny was on Global Medical's locum tenens website and found a cardiology position in New Zealand. To me it sounded like a dream job! No weekends on call, and they would supply a car and a house. Global Medical's motto was inspiring: "Go far and do good." Bonny exclaimed, "I love New Zealand and I don't mind driving on the left side of the road." I thought there was no way the move would actually happen, but we sought more details, and our journey began. Two different job opportunities presented themselves, and I decided to pursue both. To apply, I had to present my original medical degree, original board certification, medical qualifications, and multiple letters of recommendation. Then I had to complete phone interviews, travel to New Zealand, and churn through a treadmill of personal interviews.

My first in-person interview was at a hospital on the North Island that served an agricultural community of eighty thousand people, as well as thousands more district-wide. It did not offer more advanced procedures such as stenting and open-heart surgery, but referred patients needing those interventions to a hospital in Wellington, the capital of New Zealand. This position was attractive because it was a permanent job and did not require working on weekends or holidays. It did require that I obtain certification in transesophageal echocardiography, however, a skill I would need to learn.

My second interview was for a temporary six-month position on the South Island in Christchurch. At that moment, Christchurch, the largest city on the South Island, was recovering from a massive earthquake that had taken place the year prior. The earthquake had destroyed a good portion of the central business district. I remember sitting in a coffee shop on a cold morning before my interview when it started hailing outside. I watched a young student walk in wearing shorts and jandals, which is Kiwi for flip-flops, and calmly order a flat white. It became clear to me right away that the Kiwis are a hardy people.

The Christchurch job required me to be on call nights and week-ends, and it also involved reading lots and lots of echocardio-grams, or echos, as they're called, so I decided to accept the offer at the North Island hospital. I applied for a practicing certificate with the medical council of New Zealand, and then I went through clinical certification for the performance of transesophageal echo-cardiography back in the United States. I obtained a medical cer-tification approval letter, underwent a physical examination for a New Zealand work visa that involved drawing blood and obtain-ing a chest x-ray, sent passports to the embassy in Washington, DC, got visa approval, and set up an appointment for a medical council interview in Wellington.

As in the movies, calendar pages seemed to leap from the wall, and our departure date was at hand. After a lot of hard work, I was finally able to start a new life in New Zealand, where, when my colleagues wanted a gentle way to explain to one another that they had just lost a patient, they would say he or she "sucked the kumara," a phrase I found both wry and sad. The wryness helped.

———————

In New Zealand, I found people to be pragmatic, with an over-whelmingly optimistic outlook on life. They truly seemed to believe it when they said "no worries," perhaps the most common phrase I heard during my time there. There were so many positive things to enjoy in my new country that it seemed silly to worry about little hiccups. For instance, there was very little traffic, and no charge to bring your own wine at restaurants. There was no airport security for domestic flights when we left to visit other parts of the country. We found the air to be clean and the water crystal clear. The rivers and oceans were full of trout, salmon, snapper, clams, oysters, whitebait, and green-lipped mussels. The people struck me as relaxed, honest, and genuinely friendly. It was hard for me to get stressed out while living in New Zealand. "She'll be right," as the popular saying goes. Kiwis maintained that life would work out in the end, so you might as well enjoy it, and I took the assertion at face value. Eventually I came to believe that I myself would live longer as a Kiwi, and so would my patients.

I also found the practice of medicine in New Zealand to be far more humane for both patients and doctors in many ways. After moving there, I paid only $1,397.25 NZ (about $1,117 US) for an annual subscription to the Medical Protection Society, which was roughly equivalent to medical malpractice insurance in the US. In New Zealand, the Medical Protection Society offers a system of no-fault payment that "harmonizes injuries compensation, provider accountability, and patient safety." Patients in New Zealand are not eligible for compensation through malpractice suits, but rather through the Accident Compensation Corporation, a government-funded, no-fault means of addressing unintended incidents in patient care. An administrative process determines the compensation and can resolve the issue within weeks or months.

The US system for medical compensation, on the other hand, remains highly confrontational. Compensation is determined by legal actions that often treat physicians as if they are guilty of criminal negligence. These lawsuits can also take years to resolve disputes and incur enormous expenses. Each side typically needs to hire a team of medical experts, and a settlement for medical malpractice can result in 50 percent of the compensation being paid to an attorney. The US medical compensation system costs billions, whereas to date only twenty-nine million New Zealand dollars has been spent on medical injuries in New Zealand. The US also has a higher rate of patients being injured by medical errors (9.7 percent) than New Zealand does (5.6 percent), according to a 2006 article in the journal *Health Affairs*. In other words, the US system is both costly and emotionally draining for physicians and patients, and it does not improve patient safety. In fact, it leads to a culture in which physicians order excessive testing, a practice that is widely described by doctors as "cover your ass." The ubiquity of malpractice lawsuits serves the interests of lawyers more than the interests of patients or doctors.

While I was living in New Zealand, there came a moment when I realized I no longer was the same person I had been in the US. Life had changed for the better, and the formerly tense and worried version of myself—transplanted from the fraught hallways of an American hospital—had slowly eased with the passing years into a more relaxed person and thus a better doctor. If I looked closely at myself, I could name what I might call scars, but there was no longer constant inner pain. Now the scars were simply part of my story. Instead of something I ran from, the experience of being a doctor in the US seemed to be, in retrospect, responsible for a sense of strength in who I became in New Zealand. And the process of healing from searing difficulties encountered in a profession gone awry left me with the desire to share what I learned during my time in the Southern Hemisphere with everyone who was, or still is, struggling to practice medicine the right way in the United States. My hope is to foster more humane interactions between doctors and patients all around the world, particularly in so-called "developed" countries such as the US. If I could heal as an individual, couldn't the medical profession also heal itself?

Chapter Two

GROWING UP

My family story could be likened to *The Grapes of Wrath* by John Steinbeck, as it involves a migration from dust bowl-era Oklahoma to the promised land of milk and honey in southern California. Californians called people like my grandparents "Okies" when they arrived on the Pacific Coast. My grandpa once told me a story about when he first got to California and picked up a hitchhiker. The hitchhiker complained about waiting so long for a ride. "Must have been a bunch of 'Okies' out on the road today," he said. Irritated, my grandpa replied, "You just got a ride from an 'Okie.'"

Southern California was very fertile, and in the 1950s it was covered with verdant orange groves. That's where I first experienced the crisp, sweet taste of freshly squeezed orange juice. We had thirty orange trees; we also grew avocados and plums and had a boysenberry patch on our property. The streets were lined with eucalyptus trees, whose smell still reminds me of my childhood.

This was the California I was born into in 1951, where on a clear day you could stand on a golden beach and see snow-capped mountains in the distance.

Though the surroundings were idyllic, the atmosphere inside our home was not. When I was growing up, I could see that my parents were having problems with their marriage due to my dad's drinking. At times, there was physical violence between them, and we even saw my father choke our mother. My sister and I would often spend the weekends with our grandparents, whose house became a safe harbor from the stormy situation in our own home. Someone once asked me if I thought the domestic violence that I witnessed led me to want to become a healer, or the kind of person who could intervene in a medical crisis; while at the time I scoffed at the idea, there may be something to it.

My grandpa Cecil was the most influential person in my life. Cecil was superintendent of the Carmenita and Ramona schools in Los Angeles county, and he would take me to visit those schools on the weekends. I remember driving past dairy farms that gave off the pungent smell of cow manure on the way to visit the schools that he ran. My grandpa was a charismatic public speaker. Once when I went with him on a school day, I watched the kids flock around him in the school yard, hanging on to his every word. He loved to tell jokes and riddles, much to our delight. My favorite was when he would say,

> *"Now Greek and algebra,*
> *They are a cinch;*
> *There's just one thing I'd like to know:*
> *How high is up, how low is down,*
> *And when will we have snow?"*

As I lay in bed at night, my grandpa would often tell me stories about my great-grandfather, Dr. John Paul Jones, who had practiced medicine in Oklahoma back when it was still a territory.

"When your great-grandfather passed on," my grandpa once told me, "the entire town shut down to go to his funeral."

My eyes widened and I asked, "Why, Grandpa?" He smiled and said that when my great-grandfather's patients couldn't pay, he would take whatever they offered. It might be eggs, or perhaps chickens. He even took a pig once, for delivering twins.

"A pig?" I asked.

"Yes," my grandpa nodded. "Times were hard, and people didn't have money. He was a humanitarian."

I didn't know what a humanitarian was exactly, but I liked the sound of the word, and I sensed that it meant developing some capacity for doing good, which my great-grandfather had evidently possessed, and which my grandfather implied could be passed on to me. On that particular spring night, in the middle of a thunderstorm with the sound of rain pelting the window glass, I decided that my destiny was to become a doctor.

———————

I grew up in a different America than the one I see around me today. Back then, kids mowed lawns, pulled weeds, babysat, helped neighbors with chores, and had a paper route to be able to earn money. We went outside frequently to play games, ride bikes, and run around with our siblings and our friends. Unofficial baseball contests were held in the front yard. We drank water from the hose outside; none of us had ever heard of such a thing as bottled water.

We watched TV on Friday nights alone, and we savored the one coke we were allowed to drink each week. After school, we came home and did our homework and our chores before going outside or having friends over. We did not know that the word "screens" would someday apply to the phone or the computer. We rode our bikes for hours. Once the sun started to set, though, we knew we had better be home in time for dinner.

In school we had earthquake drills, said the Pledge of Allegiance, stood for the National Anthem, and listened to and respected our teachers. Ms. Anderson, my second-grade teacher, had honey-colored hair pulled up in a bun and bright red lipstick. I had a crush on her, so when she told me that she would take me out for ice cream if I got 100 percent on my spelling test, I was thrilled. Not to take any chances, I copied the ten words on a piece of paper, which I concealed at my feet below my desk.

I got one hundred on the test, and, as promised, Ms. Anderson took me out for ice cream. I was so nervous, given that I had cheated in order to get a date with my teacher, that I couldn't eat any of my treat. I sat there and watched it melt all over the front seat of her car.

When I was ten years old, I made the Little League baseball team. Our coach was very fair, making sure everyone got to play in each game, which led to great team spirit. During our last game of the season, it was the bottom of the sixth inning, the bases were loaded with nobody out, we had a one-run lead, and we were tied with the opposing team for first place in our league. In other words, whichever team won that afternoon would become the league champion. As I stood in right field, I heard the distinctive crack of the wooden bat and saw the ball sail high in the air toward shallow right field. I started to run as hard as I could and made a shoestring catch. The base runners on the opposing team had gone for broke, as it looked like the ball was going to drop in for a hit and they felt sure they were going to win the game. Instead, I  threw the ball to second, the second baseman threw to first, and we were able to tag our opponents out at both bases, in addition to the hitter being out due to the fly ball I had caught. Thanks to this triple play, we won the game and the league championship. I felt elated as my teammates pounded me on the back.

Not long after, while my grandpa was driving me to one of his schools, he told me the story of how he had walked an hour to school and back again each day, in all kinds of weather. "It was difficult, but we did it because we had a real thirst for education," he said. He also related how after he got his high school degree, he obtained a teaching certificate and took a job as a teacher in a grammar school. He then attended college classes in the summer for thirteen years, while working from fall to spring, until he got his bachelor's degree.

When he told me the story of walking an hour to school each way, I exclaimed, "I could do that, Grandpa!"—to which he replied,

"No, you are too used to riding in a car to walk that far." So, one Saturday morning, I set off with one of my Little League team-mates to walk the twelve miles to my grandpa's house from Ross-moor to Anaheim. It was a beautiful sunny day, and when we got thirsty or hungry, we would stop in one of the abundant orange groves, peel an orange, and eat it. When I arrived at my grandpa's, he asked, "Where's your mother?" When I told him I had walked, he was astonished. I felt proud of the accomplishment, as I had shown my grandpa that I could do what he thought I could not.

During my freshman year of high school, my father got transferred from our little town in southern California to Trenton, New Jersey. He was a comptroller for Transamerica and was sent there to reorganize a company they had just purchased. I went from California's blonde-haired and sun-tanned surf culture to being surrounded by pale kids with dark hair and acne in crewnecks and penny loafers. It was late fall, and biting cold, with no leaves on the trees. It got dark early, too. I was in culture shock.

I also missed my grandfather terribly, and the proximity we had enjoyed to the safe and comforting home environment he had provided. However, I soon found a substitute mentor who inspired and challenged me in a similar way. My next-door neighbor was a man named Dr. Topley, with whom I formed a friendship after spending a lot of time at his house, thanks to the fact that he had a son around my age. We would have long philosophical discussions after dinner. Dr. Topley told me, "Steve, if you really want to make a difference in life, become a doctor." One night, he told me a story about when he had been in medical school in Boston and had responded to a call from a poor family whose daughter was in labor. Despite a difficult labor, he was able to deliver the baby safely and witnessed the new mother cuddle her newborn. He said, "For the first time in my life, I felt like I had made a difference."

Later, when my beloved grandfather was visiting from California, he suffered a heart attack in the middle of the trip. While he was in our living room, lying on the couch and clutching his chest, I ran next door to get Dr. Topley. Dr. Topley took command of the situation instantly, caring for my grandpa in our living room. He administered medication to relieve Grandpa's chest pain, and he spoke in a calm and soothing manner, putting all of us at ease. Thankfully, my grandfather was able to recover quickly and lived for many more years. I never forgot witnessing that moment of vulnerability when my grandfather became incapacitated, nor Dr. Topley's caring and effective intervention. I knew then that this was indeed the type of person I most wanted to become.

I went to college at the University of Richmond, and after a slow start my freshman year, I hit my stride and started making good grades. Then I applied to medical school and, as a backup, to dental school. When I got into dental school but not medical school, I asked Dr. Topley what to do. He wisely said, "Steve, if you want to be a dentist, go to dental school, but if you want to be a doctor, go to medical school."

Dr. Topley's son, who had been my high-school classmate and was now my friend, had not gotten into medical school either. Dr. Topley advised both of us to explore schools abroad. My parents were skeptical about the credibility of this option, and worried that it seemed potentially expensive: overseas medical schools often charged non-locals exorbitant amounts to study alongside their domestic students. Dr. Topley encouraged us to consider this option seriously, however, as he believed it was a good alternative way to get started as a medical student. Spending a couple of years studying abroad, he said, was the equivalent of a side-door entry into the US education system, because one could transfer into an American medical school later, in time for the clinical phase of training. He even paid for me to go to Mexico for an interview. So, I passed on dental school in the United States and ended up enrolling in a foreign medical school based in Guadalajara, Mexico, where I roomed with Dr. Topley's son. My parents eventually became convinced that this was a good path forward as well, and agreed to pay for my tuition and expenses. I was on the way to realizing my dream.

Chapter Three

MEDICAL TRAINING TO PRIVATE PRACTICE

At first, the only impediments I encountered were the minor bureaucratic hurdles that stood between a foreign student and a medical degree. I had to get a student visa so that I could study in Mexico, for example, and upon entering the country, I was ushered into the Mexican government's immigration office and told I would have to return to the US because I didn't have the right stamp. The government official, who had slicked-back hair and a small moustache, pulled up a chair behind his desk and said that, for a favor, he could fix the visa for me so I wouldn't have to return to the US. I said OK, so he stamped my visa. "Now what are you going to do for me, *señor?*" he asked. I stood up from my chair, shook his hand, and said, "God will repay you more than I ever could." He laughed, seemingly satisfied with this improvised blessing, and I took my visa and walked out of the room.

In hindsight, I can see that obtaining part of my education abroad may have prepared me well to practice medicine outside of the United States, but this was not clear to me at the time. Like most of the expatriate students, I was determined to return to the US as swiftly as possible. There was a large group of Americans studying in Guadalajara. Dr. Topley's son was more dedicated than I, and he studied incessantly. We didn't spend much time together, as he would emerge from his room only to make a cup of coffee or gulp down a meal, and then return to his books. We didn't use the Mexican medical textbooks because they were written in Spanish, but instead found out what textbooks medical students in American schools were using and studied from those. We were supposed to attend lectures that were held in Spanish. Some of the American students skipped this obligation, and a few even paid Mexican students to go and sit in their assigned chairs, as attendance was taken by seating place, but I faithfully attended the lectures. My Spanish was at a conversational level already, and I quickly became fluent in common terms for parts of the body such as *corazón* (heart) and *pulmón* (lungs). Soon enough I discovered that I could understand most of the lectures, but I still learned a substantial amount by reading the American textbooks.

My goal was to pass Part 1 of the exam administered by the National Board of Medical Examiners, which focuses on basic scientific principles, and then transfer into an American medical school for clinical training. The program for transfer students was called the Coordinated Transfer Application System, or COTRANS. Fewer than half of those who took Part 1 of the board exam passed, and only about half of those who passed managed to transfer into a US medical school.

As I worked to master the coursework that is the basis of a good medical education, I also learned all that I could about the local environment. I was sharing an apartment with Dr. Topley's son and a friend, and the three of us pooled our money and bought a used red Volkswagen Beetle, which we used to explore the area. The neighborhood where we lived was a relatively upscale suburb of Guadalajara called Providencia. Everybody living there typically paid a small sum to a watchman who promised that we would not be robbed as long as we paid him to watch over us. We followed the custom, and we never were robbed.

A wonderful woman named Josefina came to clean our apartment several days a week, and she also cooked meals for us. My family had never had a maid or a cook, and I felt lucky that we were able to afford her help. It was the 1970s, and like many in the laboring classes at that time, Josefina worked for very low wages. As I recall we paid her something like twenty or thirty US dollars per week. Josefina had a delightful young daughter named Maria, who sometimes accompanied her mother and helped her out in various ways. Josefina would send Maria off to a nearby tortilla factory to buy freshly made, still-warm corn tortillas. I fell into the habit of going with Maria so that I could pay for the tortillas and help her carry them back. We bought one hundred tortillas at a time, and Maria used to eat four or five of them on our walk back to the apartment.

After she turned twelve, Maria got a job of her own, working as a live-in maid for a wealthy Mexican family. Josefina missed having her at home so much that one day I offered to drive her over to visit Maria. When we arrived, Maria blushed bright red and went to hide in her room, perhaps because she wasn't expecting a visit. "*María está embarazada*," I pronounced, thinking I had a good command of Spanish. Josefina burst out laughing, while the matron of the house looked aghast. I later learned the correct word for embarrassed was *avergonzada*. I had accidentally said that Maria was pregnant! I learned a lot during that time, especially from my mistakes. Going to medical school in Mexico helped me become a more humble person, as well as more aware of my own privilege as a white person of European descent who spoke English.

———

I came of age in a period when most doctors in the United States were white men, and some advantages flowed to me because of personal connections. I studied hard and passed Part 1 of the board exam, and then got a lucky break. My family had recently moved to the Shenandoah Valley, so I applied through COTRANS to transfer to a medical school in Virginia. During my interview with Dr. Norman Knorr, the Dean of the University of Virginia Medical School, he remarked, "We were born on the same day, September 9th, and your recommendation is from my best friend in the Navy!" We laughed at the coincidence, and then he said, "Wait outside while my secretary types up your acceptance letter."

I entered the University of Virginia Medical School as a third-year medical student. My dream of becoming a doctor seemed like it was finally coming true. The clinical experience at the medical school was excellent and very hands-on. We had our own lab where we collected blood samples from patients, spun the blood down, and calculated the hematocrit, or the volume of red blood cells that the blood contained. We mixed patients' sputum with gram stains that let us see the type of bacteria present, and we would then determine whether these bacteria were causing infection in the lungs. We collected urine samples and analyzed their contents, examining them through a microscope to evaluate whether bacterial infections were present in the urinary tract.

One day, I had to perform a history and physical on an elderly lady with gray hair and glasses. She was sitting up in bed reading when I walked in. I had on a short white coat over my collared shirt and tie, and a stethoscope around my neck. I introduced myself by saying, "Hi, I'm Dr. Stowers, and I'm here to take a history and physical."

She looked up, peering over her glasses, and said, "You look too young to be a doctor." Red-faced, I explained that I was a third-year medical student who was currently assigned to her case. The next day, I started to grow a moustache to make me look older, and I still have a moustache to this day.

During my clinical rotation in cardiology, I was assigned to the chief of cardiology, Dr. Julian Beckwith, an old-school Virginia gentleman. After seeing an elderly patient with end-stage heart disease, the house officer suggested that we perform an invasive procedure. Dr. Beckwith replied, "No: when someone gets up into their 80s, the less you do to them, the more you do for them." It was good advice that has served me well throughout the years. I can't speak to the quality of medical education within American hospitals today, but as a student in the 1970s, I learned that a conservative approach often benefited patients, and there was never once a discussion about how a procedure might affect the revenue of the institution.

I also witnessed transformative changes in medicine, such as the beginning of greater gender equality in healthcare. I remember quite vividly my time in plastic surgery. Dr. Milton Edgerton was one of the few surgeons in the country performing sex-reassignment operations, in which he changed the sexual organs from those of a male into those of a female. The patient first got a psychological evaluation, hormone therapy, and breast implants. Dr. Edgerton would then perform genital conversion, turning the penis into a vagina, which was a long and complex operation. I remember watching him dissect the penis and invert the scrotum to create a vagina. This type of procedure was controversial at the time, but studies showed that most of the patients were grateful for the surgery and led happier lives afterwards.

American society itself was going through a dramatic upheaval, though I was so busy that I was slow to appreciate this fact. I spent so many hours learning all I could while simultaneously caring for patients that I did not socialize very often. One night, however, I was invited to a party of psychology graduate students, and since I didn't have transportation and the party was out in the countryside, one of them offered to pick me up. When I got in the car, the young woman in the front seat turned around and said, with mock surprise, "Are you wearing cologne?" I had spent the last three years sitting at a desk reading medical textbooks, and I didn't realize that natural body scent was now in vogue. At the party, I ended up being cornered by a group of advocates for rape victims, who wanted to know why they weren't granted more access to patients in the emergency department. I explained that I was just a third-year medical student and hadn't even rotated through the emergency department yet. Later I would come to understand their concerns when I learned that they were trying to advocate for young students who were victims of rape, and who should have been treated better during their medical examinations. At the time, however, I felt slightly intimidated by the outspoken advocates I had just met. It made me realize how much society had changed since I had been away for three years, studying in Mexico.

While in Virginia, I was finding my path forward in medicine, and finding the path to starting a family of my own, too. The grad happy hour was hosted by the graduate student union, which backed in beer trucks and unloaded kegs onto the gymnasium floor. Payment was based on the honor system, so you put your money in a box next to the keg, and then poured yourself a beer. It was there that I met a Russian-language major named Olga, with whom I became instantly infatuated and later married. I liked her because she was smart, with a quick wit and a good sense of humor. We turned out to be two very different people, however, and the marriage only lasted a couple of months. I had not yet found the right person with whom to settle down permanently.

Graduation from medical school was one of the happiest days of my life. I was beaming with pride as I marched down the lawn with the graduating class of 1978. I gave Dean Knorr a big hug when he handed me my diploma.

Once I finished medical school, I needed to move to Missouri to do an internship at the University of Missouri-Kansas City. My dad helped me drive out in a yellow Nissan that I got for graduation. The trip took about three days, and everything was going well until we were about halfway, when my father started drinking. All the bad memories from my childhood came flooding back: having to drag him out of bars and drive him home, watching him fight with my mother. When we got to Kansas City, my dad helped me move into a furnished apartment near the Nelson Art Gallery, and then he flew back home the next day. I was grateful for his help, despite the complications caused by his drinking.

Even though I was only in my mid-twenties, within the medical world I now assumed enormous responsibility. As an intern, after rounds, I was on my own in terms of treating patients, with the exception of a pharmacist who stayed on call to advise doctors-in-training on the proper use of pharmaceuticals. The pharmacist I worked with was a young man named Bobby Curtis from Quincy, Massachusetts, and he had a thick Boston accent. I remember one night on call when we had a woman in critical care whose low blood pressure would not respond to dopamine, an IV medication used to bring up blood pressure. Bobby called the pharmaceutical company to get approval for compassionate use of dobutamine, a newly developed agent that was even more powerful than dopamine. He was successful, and the Missouri State Police delivered the medicine to us within the hour. With the excitement and anticipation of being among the first medical professionals to use this new agent, we started the IV infusion, only to see the patient's blood pressure drop further. We stopped the infusion, and her blood pressure came up. The next time we restarted the infusion, the same thing happened: her blood pressure dropped yet again. We later came to understand the patient had low blood pressure from a bloodstream infection called sepsis that causes maximal dilatation of the arteries and low blood pressure. While dobutamine improves the strength of heart contractions and can thereby help raise blood pressure, it also has properties that dilate the arteries, which in this patient's case dropped the blood pressure further. The patient's blood pressure improved once her sepsis was identified and she began IV antibiotics.

Learning from clinical experience means being able to say: I won't make that mistake again. Today, many American doctors live in dire fear of admitting mistakes, given the prevalence of lawsuits, but in truth becoming a doctor involves making many good decisions and the occasional wrong one due to unforeseeable circumstances. One learns from those errors, and the act of doing so is a key part of the acquisition of clinical experience. A culture in which one can neither make nor admit mistakes is not a healthy atmosphere.

Another noteworthy incident occurred when I was assigned to the emergency room. We used to get a lot of inner-city traumas, and they called our unit "the knife and gun club." One evening, a young man presented with a stab wound to the chest. He proceeded quickly into cardiac arrest, and a nurse called a code. My job on the code team was to obtain an ECG to detect the pattern of his heart's electrical activity. As I entered the room, I saw a young man lying unconscious with a large kitchen knife protruding from the left side of his chest. I had never seen anything like this before and can still recall the shock I felt at the sight of that big knife in his body. Nothing I had studied in medical school had prepared me for this harsh clinical reality.

I plugged in the ECG machine and a surgical resident began pumping on the man's chest, but what the patient really needed was for his chest to be cracked open and the bleeding stopped. Soon the surgical team whisked the patient off to surgery to repair the knife wound. The patient didn't survive, but I had learned a critical lesson. Not all cardiac arrest patients need a heart tracing, even though this is standard procedure. Sometimes you simply have to jump into action, crack open the chest, and stop the bleeding from a knife wound.

———————

Following my internship, I decided to pursue cardiology and completed my two years of residency at a Yale-affiliated hospital in Danbury, Connecticut. My fondest memory of residency was making rounds at Yale New Haven Hospital with the world-renowned clinician Howard Spiro. One time he asked me to examine a patient who had a high-pitched systolic murmur and an enlarged liver that pulsated against my fingers when I pressed down on the abdomen. Dr. Spiro asked me what was causing the liver to pulsate. My mind went blank, as I had never seen a patient with a pulsating liver. Dr. Spiro smiled and gently explained that it was from tricuspid regurgitation. With each heartbeat, a valve on the right side of the heart called the tricuspid was leaking a jet of blood back into the liver, causing it to pulsate. Given that cardiology was my field of endeavor, I was embarrassed not to have known the answer, but afterward I felt determined to learn everything I could about tricuspid regurgitation. Dr. Spiro was an inspiration as a clinician and as a bedside teacher because he was able to transfer what we learned while reading about a disease to a real-life, in-person clinical presentation.

I chose to specialize in cardiology because I felt that was where the action was. Treating the heart was exciting and dynamic. Patients showed up exhibiting fast heartbeats, slow heartbeats, high blood pressure, and low blood pressure, meaning the clinical presentation was always changing. And perhaps I was influenced by having seen Dr. Topley save my grandfather's life when my grandfather had a heart attack in our living room. I hoped to become a person who, like Dr. Topley, could intervene successfully in the middle of an acute crisis.

Danbury, Connecticut is also where I met my wife-to-be, Bonny. We found each other at a Halloween party that took place dur-

ing my residency, while bob-
bing for apples. She asked if
I could give her a ride home,
and on the way we stopped
at a railroad crossing. As the
train rumbled by, I let her
bucket seat down and kissed
her. Bonny has beautiful
brown eyes, a heartwarm-
ing smile, and a wonderful
sense of humor, and I fell in

love with her straight away. We dated throughout the rest of my
medical education. After completing my residency, I moved to
Portland, Maine, where I worked in cardiology at Maine Medical
Center, with the hope of becoming a primary-care cardiologist.
When that year was done, however, I decided that I wanted more
extensive training, so I began a two-year cardiology fellowship at
George Washington University Hospital in Washington, DC.

I remember our chief of cardiology, Dr. Allan Ross, leading the
weekly review of coronary angiograms we had performed during the week. The patients' clinical histories, electrocardiograms,
echocardiograms, and stress tests would all be put together.
"With inferior ECG changes on stress test, what coronary artery
do you expect to be involved, Steve?" asked Dr. Ross, at one of
these gatherings.

"Narrowing in the right coronary artery which supplies the inferior wall," I replied. He made it all coherent, and it was a good
learning experience.

Bonny was still living in Connecticut, and she would drive down to see me on the weekends. One weekend, the area had a severe snowstorm, and we cross-country skied down Wisconsin Avenue to the Washington Monument. Her car was buried in the snow for a week before we were able to dig it out. We got married that June, right after I finished my fellowship. Bobby Curtis, my pharmacist friend from Kansas City, flew east to serve as my best man, and then Bonny and I moved down to Florida, where I took a job with the University of Florida in Jacksonville.

Jacksonville is in northeast Florida, near the state line with Georgia, and it has a Southern conservative vibe. In 1984, the area still featured the distinctive odor of sulfur emanating from the papermill processing plants. I worked at the indigent-care hospital, University Hospital, which saw Jacksonville's inner-city population, predominantly low-income people of color. One young African-American woman stood out as such an unusual case that I later published her presentation in the *American Heart Journal*. She had presented with exertional chest pain to a local cardiologist, who had struggled to understand the cause of her discomfort. Why would a young woman in her twenties, with no risk factors for heart disease, have shown up experiencing typical exertional angina—or, in other words, an inadequate blood flow to her heart, causing an oppressive pain in her chest?

A coronary angiogram was performed, which showed that her left main coronary artery was severely narrowed. The local cardiologist had referred her to a community hospital for open-heart surgery, during which the surgeon found a large heart tumor externally compressing the left main coronary artery. The mass was "unresectable because of its involvement of the left atrium," the surgeon wrote. The tumor was biopsied but left in place, the arteries were bypassed with venous grafts, and the chest was closed. She continued to have chest pain afterward, however, and that was when she saw me for a second opinion. "I don't feel any better after the heart surgery," she said, severely disappointed with this outcome. I listened to her chest. I heard a *whoosh, whoosh*—the sound of a loud murmur. This suggested to me that a heart valve was involved.

Part of the mystery was solved when we found the heart tumor was resulting in an overproduction of adrenaline, which was speeding up her heartbeat and causing palpitations and chest pain. I started the patient on medication to block the high levels of adrenaline and was able to find a surgeon who had experience removing these types of heart tumors, known as pheochromo-cytomas. The patient then had a successful total removal of the tumor and reconstruction of the involved cardiac structures, including replacement of her mitral valve. She recovered well from that second surgery, and I saw her every year after that. I got to know her so well that I went to her wedding, and then I watched her enjoy having a daughter who grew up and later had her own daughter. Thanks to the intervention that we managed to provide, my patient was able to survive a complicated heart impairment, live a long life, and become a grandmother. This was one of the great rewards of being a cardiologist: I got to witness the positive fruits of my endeavors. For this reason above all else, I loved the years I spent in the practice of medicine.

———————

Yet medicine was changing swiftly, and I evolved, too. One major factor involved the development of new techniques, which neces-sitated expensive equipment and led to the creation of complex subspecialties. The field of interventional cardiology led the way in terms of arterial catheter-based procedures, while the field of electrophysiology pioneered the implantation of defibrillators and ever more complex pacemakers. By various means, cardiologists were accomplishing more and more without having to resort to open-heart surgery.

While still at University Hospital, I became an expert in nuclear cardiology, a subspecialty that involves using radioactive substances to do advanced imaging of the heart and the body's blood flow. One day, I ran into Gene Page, who was in a successful cardiology practice with an excellent reputation at a local hospital. "How would you like to develop a nuclear cardiology practice at my hospital?" he asked. I said yes and soon joined Gene at his hospital, only to find out three days after I began that the clinic had purchased the institution and would be taking over its administration.

Even though the clinic is a nonprofit organization with a strong reputation, many physicians worried it would push those of us with private practices out of the hospital. "He who has the gold makes the rules," I heard one physician say. The clinic, however, supported my effort to develop nuclear cardiology at the hospital. I was able to do innovative clinical research and published medical articles on the imaging of chest pain patients in the emergency department. As co-director of nuclear cardiology, I was even given a clinic email account, which made me feel like part of the team. In the long run, Gene Page ended up leaving our private practice and becoming a clinic physician, and I ended up taking over the private cardiology practice that he had helped develop.

During my time in private practice, I had one very bad experi-ence involving an accusation of malpractice. We were constantly aware of the potential to be drawn into a lawsuit if a patient had a dire outcome, so we made a point to keep up good relation-ships with our patients and to communicate openly with them and their families. One of my senior partners referred to me a diabetic patient with a subendocardial infarction, or a small heart attack, so that I could perform a coronary angiogram.

The angiogram showed that the right coronary artery had severe fatty cholesterol deposits. This patient was not a good candidate for routine balloon angioplasty because of the ulcerated nature of the lesions, but there was a new technique called directional coronary atherectomy, or DCA for short, in which cholesterol deposits could be shaved with a cutting device and then removed from the artery. I asked a colleague who had been trained in the procedure to review the films and see if the patient was a good candidate for DCA.

The next day, my colleague and I spoke with the patient and his wife about this new procedure and the risks involved; we also arranged for an open-heart surgery as backup in case anything went wrong. The patient signed the consent form, and we went ahead with the procedure. I scrubbed in on the case with my col-league and felt optimistic about achieving a successful outcome, but as we were pushing the device down the artery, cholesterol deposits became dislodged downstream, obstructing blood flow to the heart muscle. Despite his best efforts, my colleague was unable to reestablish normal flow in the artery.

I reviewed the situation with the open-heart surgeon who had been called to the cath lab, and after looking at the images while sitting on the counter in his surgical scrubs, the surgeon said, "Steve, he has embolized cholesterol plaque distally—coronary bypass surgery isn't going to help him now." In other words, the artery was now blocked so far downstream, the surgeon would not be able to bypass the obstruction. The patient continued to have low blood pressure due to damage to his right ventricle; he didn't respond to treatment, and unfortunately died the next day. I felt terrible. It was the first time I'd had a patient die as the result of an intervention.

What transpired next is part of the story of what is wrong, in my opinion, with American medicine. The patient's family sued and got an expert to say that we should have referred him to coronary bypass surgery to address the compromised artery. Our lawyers hired experts who defended our position. We underwent sworn depositions, our experts were deposed, and their experts were deposed. Two years later, my colleague ended up settling the case. I refused to settle and went to a jury trial.

At the first day of the trial, the prosecution showed a picture of the deceased patient with his family during the winter holidays. "Because of this doctor's negligence," the prosecutor announced, "this family will never have another Christmas together." The statement struck me like a thunderbolt. I had always thought of myself as a healer, a good doctor who helped people get better. Now I was being portrayed as an incompetent physician whose negligence had led to a person's death. I could not steady myself until I got home, where I heartened myself by looking at a framed picture of my family under our own Christmas tree. By this point Bonny and I had four children, who depended upon me to provide for them. I told myself I had to persevere.

The trial felt like a circus. It came out that a nurse in the cath lab had told her husband about the case, and he had then referred it to his fishing buddy, a malpractice lawyer. The wife of the deceased patient testified that I had never discussed the risks inherent in the procedure with her, contradicting her deposition in which she said under sworn oath that I had indeed discussed the procedure with her. The "expert witness," as it turned out, was being paid $20,000 a day for his testimony, and his claim to be an expert on DCA was based on the fact that during medical school he had been the roommate of the developer of the DCA procedure, John Simpson. We won the case, but the entire process took two full years, and while our legal bills were covered by insurance, I was left emotionally drained by the experience and disillusioned with American malpractice. This was not merely a personal setback, but part of a vast trend of vilifying doctors for monetary gain when patients encounter setbacks. In the years from 1990 to 2002, the number of malpractice payments made annually in Florida rose almost tenfold, and across that span of time amounted to a total of over $3 billion in that state alone.

Despite the terrible lawsuit we endured, local general practitioners who made referrals to us stayed loyal, and our practice grew. One family practitioner, Buster Browning, was especially supportive and soon I was able to hire two additional colleagues and build a thriving business. One thing that I loved about my practice was that we often saw several patients from the same families—parents and grandparents, aunts and uncles, cousins and nephews who had all been coming to us for years. I was able to build close personal relationships with my patients over long periods of time, and I would often go to the birthday parties and weddings of people whom I had seen as patients. I remember a spunky lady from Brooklyn who would give me advice on disciplining my son: "If he doesn't behave, pop him!" she would say. I had a Filipino patient who would come in and fry lumpia in the kitchen of our office right after his appointment. Another patient brought us fresh fruits and vegetables from the market he ran. As Christmas approached, the office tables would fill up with nuts, candy, and fruit from the patients. We would have the office holiday party at my house, and everyone from the office would bring their spouses and celebrate the season together. Patients, nurses, technicians, and doctors shared a closeness born from facing serious issues together, and we functioned like a large extended clan. Even my wife Bonny helped out in the office as a volunteer. She assisted with managing the financial side of the practice and greeted patients when they arrived. Our nurse practitioner would make us all laugh, saying our practice had "good juju."

Unexpectedly, this era of my life came to an abrupt close when the clinic announced they were building their own hospital in the same area. As a result, they would be selling the local hospital that had hosted my private practice to a large healthcare corporation, taking our certificate-of-need for a heart program to their new hospital. The certificate had been issued by the state, giving its approval to the operation of certain programs within the local facility. This was the kind of reorganization I had feared, for changes like this were happening across the United States, with hundreds of smaller local institutions being subsumed into ever-larger for-profit corporations, or big non-profit organizations like the clinic. I organized the community's physicians, and in 2003 and we were able to pass legislation that saved the heart program at the local hospital. This remains one of my proudest achievements: working together with other local medical professionals to prevent the loss of a vital service to the community.

The clinic was not the most problematic institution in the field, but to me it represented the pronounced shift from local control to control by regional or national organizations. When the clinic left our hospital, they took all the best nurses and technicians with them to the new institution. The departure of experienced staff created a leadership void, and patient care suffered. The reputation of the local hospital waned, and patients and referring physicians started leaving. The cost of malpractice insurance also skyrocketed due to the increasing prevalence of expensive lawsuits, and the reimbursements our hospital's physicians received began to decline. This was particularly prevalent in the burgeoning field of cardiac imaging, where, according to a study published in the *New England Journal of Medicine*, reimbursements for outpatient imaging were slashed by up to 40 percent, largely to prevent cardiologists from self-referring and performing imaging on their own patients. For this reason, many independent cardiology practices had to join forces with hospitals, which would allow them to be compensated for imaging at twice the outpatient rate. I was known nationally for my expertise in nuclear cardiology and had many referrals for those procedures, but the amount I was reimbursed for each procedure dropped dramatically over time, until it was only a fraction of what I had once received. Forced by financial circumstances to abandon my private practice, I began negotiations with the new hospital administration to sell the practice and become a hospital-employed physician. Working directly for the new hospital resulted in diminishing joy in my work—I only lasted nineteen months.

Over the years I spent in private practice, I had become more and more enthusiastic about the power of diet, medication, and lifestyle changes to halt the progression of coronary artery disease. Americans eat a diet high in saturated fat, which clogs their coronary arteries and leads to four hundred thousand coronary bypass operations and two million coronary stent placements being performed each year in the United States. In patients with high levels of problematic cholesterol, studies have shown that cholesterol-lowering statins can reduce cardiovascular events by 22 percent. Studies have also shown that patients can reduce their risk for cardiovascular events by up to 50 percent through beneficial changes in lifestyle. I had read a wonderful book by the preventive-medicine expert Dean Ornish on reversing heart disease through diet, and I also took some of my patients to the Wellspring Wellness retreat in Silverton, Oregon, for a weeklong immersion program in stress reduction, meditation, low-fat dieting, and daily exercise. I was convinced that if we didn't turn off the faucet of cholesterol and prevent the sink from overflowing, so to speak, we would be continually mopping up excess fat in the coronary arteries with stents and coronary bypass surgeries. As long as I had been working for myself, I had been able to advise my patients to try non-invasive methods of improving their health, and it had worked. Once I began working for the hospital, however, I was encouraged to conduct more invasive interventions.

While still working for the new administration, I thought—naively—that perhaps I could influence the hospital. With the support of one of the hospital's major donors, I approached the administration with the idea of starting our own wellness clinic like the one I had attended in Oregon. They agreed to let us speak to the hospital's other donors, and a luncheon was set up. During my speech at the luncheon, I pointed out that recent heart studies had shown that coronary stents do not prolong life or prevent heart attacks. What was really needed was to turn off the supply of cholesterol to prevent it from building up in the coronary arteries, and thus to avoid the cause of debilitating heart attacks and deaths in the first place. Then I presented my idea for a wellness center. The wife of one of the cardiologists stood up and walked out. Her husband was number one on the administration's list of coronary stents placed; my idea was dead on arrival. From where I stood, it seemed as though the hospital's administrators didn't want to cure heart disease; they just wanted to maintain the status quo. Let cholesterol blockages continue to build up, and more stents would be placed inside of patients, and millions of dollars in revenue would be realized. I could not believe in the hospital's leaders anymore, and they did not believe in me. My attempt to practice medicine in a way that would allow me to become the kind of humanitarian my great-grandfather had been clashed with the priorities of the "suits" who were tracking stent placements as a primary measure of success. I thought those costly interventions should rather be considered a measure of failure: failure to achieve early diagnosis and treat the patient through more helpful and non-invasive means. The hospital parted ways with me, and I began to look for a new job.

Yet all around the country, the same major trends prevailed. When I started out as a practitioner in the 1980s, 72 percent of American physicians were in private practice, and in the area where I worked in northeast Florida, all the hospitals were independent, community-based institutions. Today, all hospitals serving the same area are part of national or regional entities, while the number of physicians in private practice has dropped below 50 percent. In my field, it had once been common for cardiologists to practice internal medicine as well and to know everything about their patients. We would admit our patients to the hospital, follow their progress while they were there, and serve as their primary care doctors, meaning that we were able to build lasting relationships with the individuals we treated. With fewer physicians in private practice, however, it became increasingly typical for hospital-employed physicians to admit patients and for the doctors who treated them to focus narrowly on particular subspecialties, leading to multiple providers participating in the care of a single patient. In my opinion, this made it harder for any one of those doctors to see the whole person, leading to the loss of a holistic approach to medical care and a sensitivity toward the human aspect of medicine. From a patient's perspective, one ended up being cared for by strangers. American medicine was caught up in a spiral of change that seemed to lead further and further away from what was moral, right, and good for patients. Bonny could see the big picture perhaps even better than I, for it was she who suggested at this point that I step outside of American medicine entirely, in order to feel whole again.

Chapter Four

STARTING OVER

Moving to New Zealand gave me the chance to start over, and while I was there, I met other doctors who had also sought refuge in its more humane medical system. Once again, we could practice medicine as we believed was right without the fear of being needlessly sued or worrying about how many RVUs we were generating. I could rely on my own clinical common sense to formulate care plans for my patients, instead of being pressured by revenue-seeking business experts to do procedures that I did not believe would benefit patients to the same degree. One of my first patients in clinic was a wonderful, vibrant, and energetic forty-four-year-old male. He looked like the picture of health. When I reviewed his medical history, I was shocked to discover that he had had a heart attack six years prior, followed by multiple stents and coronary bypass surgery at the age of forty-two. He was quite young to have had these brushes with serious medical difficulty, but he did have two risk factors: a positive family history of premature coronary atherosclerosis and an elevated serum cholesterol.

After I heard him tell his story, I calmly explained that his heart disease was treatable, but he would have to follow a rigorous diet and exercise regime and take medication to lower his cholesterol. The patient and his wife seemed happy and relieved to hear that this was all that would be required, since his wife had been worried that he was doomed to an early death. I explained that the diet was difficult to follow, as he would need to cut fat out of his diet completely, and only about 20 percent of patients are typically able to comply. I reviewed the scientific work of cardiologists Caldwell Esselstyn and Dean Ornish with him to illustrate that if he could follow my advice, the effects would be dramatic. "A diet free of fat will allow you to see your grandchildren grow up," I explained.

When I saw this patient next, he admitted he was not implementing the diet perfectly, but we saw a big drop in his cholesterol anyway thanks to the medication. In the United States, the tendency would have been to perform procedural interventions, because these are more profitable. In New Zealand, however, the hospitals are not funded by fees from patients and insurance companies, but rather by taxpayers, which means they have limited resources and must operate by a different priority system. In other words, a patient has to exhibit more advanced symptoms in order to qualify for either an angiogram or a stent. This approach is backed up by the available research, which demonstrates that non-invasive approaches make the most sense when symptoms are less advanced. For the first time in quite a while, nobody was pressuring me to perform a certain number of procedures, and I could treat my patients as I felt was appropriate, with treatments being data-driven instead of profit-driven. I was pleased with the outcome we achieved in this patient's case.

In cardiology, New Zealand doctors commonly use a system called Clinical Priority Access Criteria, or CPAC for short, to determine the urgency of referral to a tertiary care center for open-heart surgery. If a patient's CPAC score is high, he or she is moved up the list and receives open-heart surgery right away, ideally within forty-eight hours. By contrast, a lower priority patient may have to wait ninety days for open-heart surgery. New Zealand's health-care system graded patients based on their needs and aimed at a fair distribution of limited resources, and it prioritized the ability of clinicians to find solutions that were less invasive as often as possible. For the most part, patients who were stable were treated less aggressively in New Zealand than they might have been in the United States, where a patient who had shown up with chest pain can receive an angiogram and coronary bypass surgery even if their condition has stabilized and the chest pain has resolved with non-invasive treatment. I found the way of practicing medicine in New Zealand instantly refreshing, and experienced a renewed joy and fulfillment in my profession. I knew right away that I had found a place where I could practice medicine using a less aggressive and more holistic approach.

Meanwhile, outside of the hospital setting, we made friends swiftly, as people in New Zealand showed Bonny and me an extraordinary degree of warmth and hospitality. Upon our arrival in the community where I was going to practice, the local hospital administration introduced us to a nurse who had started a bed-and-breakfast in the nearby town of Feilding. We stayed there while we adjusted to being in a new country on the other side of the world. Feilding is a small city, with a population just shy of eighteen thousand. When we arrived there in 2013, it had no traffic lights, and had recently been voted the friendliest place in the country. The owners of the bed-and-breakfast were great examples of New Zealand hospitality. Reena and John were consistently friendly, and soon we were swapping recipes and cooking together. One day they asked if we wanted to have tea with them, so we were surprised when we sat down and they started serving food—"tea," we realized, means dinner in New Zealand! Reena and John also shared fresh eggs from their chickens and vegetables from their garden, and allowed us to use their clothesline to dry our clothes. I like people who get excited about the change of seasons, the sounds of the ocean, watching a sunset, the smell of rain, and starry nights. Reena and John were both that kind of person.

A member of the hospital staff introduced us to another couple in Feilding who were planning to travel to the United Kingdom and Africa for five weeks. They offered to let us stay at their home while they were gone, which gave us the opportunity to search for a place of our own at our leisure. We grew very fond of their warm house with its heated floors and felt reluctant to leave, as many of the homes we looked at were not insulated and did not have central heating. We hoped to find a place that was equally cozy, since winter would soon arrive in New Zealand, but we wound up renting a home that was without central heating but was close to the hospital, simply for the sake of convenience. While inside, I would put on a down vest to stay warm.

In the weeks before I started work at the hospital, while we were still getting settled, Bonny and I traveled to see the surrounding area. Our youngest son Jeffery was studying in London and was able to visit during his spring break. It was great to see him, as it eased the feeling of being far away from everyone we knew. We had often gone sailing as a family, and when Jeffery arrived we went sailing in the Bay of Islands, another way to help us feel at home. We chartered a forty-foot Leopard Catamaran sailboat at Opua Wharf and sailed around the many islands in the bay. Jeffery was first mate, and Bonny was chief cook and bottle washer. One day in the late afternoon, we anchored and fished for dinner. Bonny had made a vegetarian sausage that no one liked, so she used that for bait and caught a huge snapper, which we had for supper. The next day we went to another island, anchored in an inlet, and then took the dinghy ashore so we could go hiking. Jeffery and Bonny chose a different route that led inland, while I explored the coastline and promptly got lost. Every inlet looked the same, and not one contained our boat. Finally, I found an inlet with a dock and a bar. After a few drinks, I was able to borrow a map to find the inlet in which our boat was anchored. Jeffery and Bonny were extremely glad to see me when I finally returned.

Soon after our sailing trip, I went to the hospital for orientation. Orientation included a Māori ceremony known as a *pōwhiri*, a spiritual ceremony that signifies two groups coming together in a sacred act. After friendly intentions had been established, our hosts called us into the room with a traditional Māori chant and began a formal welcome of guests by the *tangata whenua*, or the people of the land. The Māori leader, who was from the community the hospital served, performed the ceremony, in which he acknowledged the support and love of his ancestors and then the sacred mountains, rivers, and lakes that make up this region of New Zealand. After singing a song together, we all lined up facing one another, and I went down the line pressing my nose to the noses of my new colleagues in a gesture called a *hongi*, while exchanging what are called *ha*, or breaths of life. I found this traditional Māori ceremony amazing and spiritually uplifting—a moving welcome to Aotearoa, as New Zealand is called by the Māori.

Historically, Māori culture has been marked by a lack of trust in western medicine and in the *P*ākehā, or white New Zealander. This skepticism dates back to the 1840 Treaty of Waitangi, through which the British Crown was granted all rights and powers of sovereignty over the land, including the ability to buy Māori land. My first experience with this distrust came about when I saw a Māori gentleman in the cardiology clinic. He was in his fifties and heavyset, with curly black hair. I found him waiting anxiously on the exam table when I entered the room. It was his first time in our clinic; he had a daughter who had insisted that he come in and get checked out. She was worried because he had been recently diagnosed with an irregular rapid heartbeat called atrial fibrillation. I took a history from him and gave him a standard physical exam, then explained that because of his heart's irregular rhythm, he was at risk of a clot forming in his heart and traveling to his brain, causing a stroke. To prevent clot formation, he needed to be on a blood thinner called Coumadin, which also goes by the generic name warfarin. He seemed to accept everything I was saying, so I continued explaining that he would also need blood tests and an echocardiogram of his heart. This would tell us whether he was a good candidate for cardioversion, an intervention in which we would produce an electric shock across his chest to try to return his heart to a normal rhythm. The patient nodded his head during my explanation of his care plan, so I thought we were communicating well. I gave him a prescription for warfarin and spoke to his GP about obtaining a referral to hematology so they could monitor his use of the blood thinner. Then I asked him to wait while I got him a pamphlet on warfarin. When I returned to the exam room, he was gone. Carol, the cardiology clinic nurse, who was Māori herself, told me the patient had left abruptly, exclaiming, "I'm not taking that rat poison."

Only then did I realize that I had not earned my patient's trust. I had spoken in a technical manner, which he must have found off-putting. I needed better communication skills, which I would work to acquire over the next six-and-a-half years. Carol became one of the primary people who helped me become a better communicator. Carol was a generous soul. She was warm-hearted and almost always looking on the bright side. I do not know what difficulties she may have endured in her own life, but in the hospital setting I never once saw her get flustered. I deeply appreciated her calm and steady presence. Often, she was the person who would come talk with me when she thought I had a tough day. She would make sure to swing by if I had a difficult case that did not resolve easily and would reassure me that I had done everything a doctor could have done. At the same time, she was also willing to explain to me what had transpired from a patient's point of view, as when my patient had fled, fearful of the "rat poison" he assumed I was prescribing. I appreciated this as well as her good cheer, because we cannot learn what we do not know unless we are told. Our paths did not have to cross in any significant way in the clinic—Carol's job was to take patients' vital signs, obtain a list of their medications, and perform ECGs in order to prepare patients to meet with me—but she extended herself and took the time to double back and offer either encouragement or a story that would stay with me as a hard piece of advice.

Another Māori belief is the idea that physical health is closely connected to spiritual health. In 2013, a prominent Māori psychiatrist named Sir Mason Durie delivered a lecture at our hospital that drove this point home. When he was in training at our same hospital, Dr. Durie told us, a fourteen-year-old Māori girl had come to a clinic with several days' history of behavioral changes at her school. When the local general practitioner heard about her visual hallucinations and strange speech, he wanted to have her committed to a mental institution. When she subsequently developed fever, headaches, delirium, and a stiff neck, however, she was brought to the emergency department and admitted to the hospital. After a thorough workup, the consultant in charge diagnosed her with viral encephalitis. The girl's grandfather, however, told the doctor that the problem wasn't a virus but a *mākutu*, a curse. He said that the girl's mother had left her behind and gone to Australia with another man, and that the girl's father's family had taken their revenge by placing a *mākutu* on his granddaughter. "That sounds a little hard to believe," the doctor had replied. "An illness such as this does not develop because of an unseen curse or mysterious force." Anti-inflammatory drugs and antiviral treatment were initiated by the hospital, while the grandfather spent every day at his granddaughter's bedside, bringing leaves of *kawakawa*, *karamu*, and *kōwhai* to heal her spirit.

"The treatment has been successful, and she has recovered from the virus," said the doctor one morning, while on rounds. The grandfather stepped forward and corrected the doctor: "My granddaughter has recovered because the curse has been lifted." The grandfather then asked the doctor, "What did the virus look like?" The doctor had to admit that he had never actually seen the virus—nor had he been able to confirm the presence of a specific pathogen. Rather, he had interpreted the girl's symptoms as fitting the pattern of a viral infection and had treated her accordingly. The grandfather smiled and said, "Doctor, I admire your faith in the power of invisible forces, in something you have never seen."

In Dr. Durie's opinion, the girl's grief and anxiety after the loss of her mother in her daily life had led to suppression of her immune system and a subsequent illness. Her case illustrated the inextricability of the health of both body and soul from one another. Dr. Durie urged us to remember the need to "recognize spirituality as part of the journey to wellness." I never forgot this powerful message.

About one-tenth of my colleagues were Māori, and the cardiology group included people from many other backgrounds. Our team included doctors from Iceland, Malaysia, South Africa, and England. I had never before worked in such a diverse environment and found it constantly enlightening. Our head nurse was Māori too, and he helped us understand Māori culture better, constantly reiterating a need for cultural sensitivity within medicine. One foundational Māori belief that he taught us, for example, is that no one should die alone, and I soon got used to the sight of a dozen or more family members gathered around the bed of a sick patient.

At the same time, the environment on the cardiology floor remained as fast-paced and exciting as it had been back in the United States. One morning, soon after the lecture by Dr. Durie, we arrived in the medical assessment and planning unit to find a concerned nurse who told us that our new patient had a heart rate of 220 beats per minute. The patient was stable and in no acute distress, so we gave him an intravenous dose of adenosine to see if we could block conduction of the rapid rhythm and thereby slow his heart rate down. The patient blocked down to a heart rate of 55 beats per minute with clear atrial flutter waves on the monitor. Due to the short half-life of intravenous adenosine, however, he quickly reverted to his prior state, and as the medication wore off, his heart rate shot back up to 220 beats per minute. We discussed sedating him with an intravenous dose of midazolam and shocking him with fifty joules across the chest at the bedside to convert his heartbeat into a normal sinus rhythm. Per hospital protocol, we called anesthesiology first; they said they wanted him taken to the operating room so that he could be intubated and his airway protected, since he had just eaten

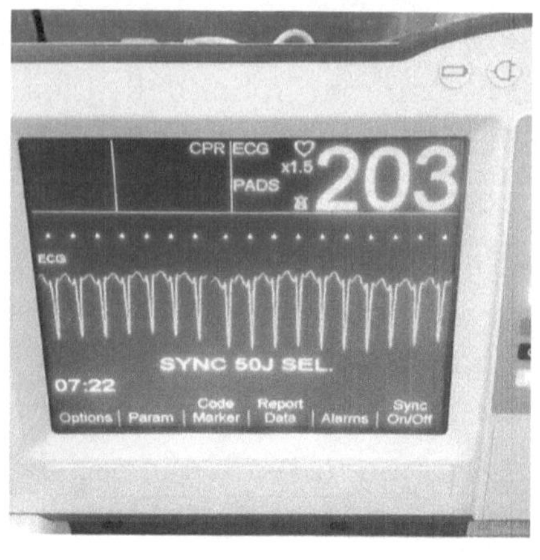

Monitor showing heart rhythm synced to 50 joules ready to shock

breakfast. In the meantime, we started an infusion of an intravenous dose of amiodarone, an antiarrhythmic medication, and then it was off to the OR for urgent cardioversion.

After we changed into scrubs, we entered the operating room in time to see the anesthesia staff administering a milky white sedative called propofol and preparing to intubate the patient. We quickly hooked him up to the biphasic cardioversion device, placed the paddles on his chest, synced to the ECG trace, and set it to deliver fifty joules of electrical current. I looked over and saw his blood pressure had dropped to an alarmingly low level, down to seventy systolic, and said that we better shock him back to normal sinus rhythm now. The cardiology registrar shouted "clear," hit the button to discharge the electrical current across the chest, and the patient immediately returned to a sinus rhythm rate of seventy beats per minute. His blood pressure returned to normal, and we were off to finish rounds. I found the work always stimulating, as each day brought new challenges.

———

The process of adjusting to the local culture took place both inside and outside of the hospital. Shortly after we arrived in New Zealand, my colleagues mentioned that they were going to celebrate something called ANZAC Day, which is a big deal in New Zealand. ANZAC stands for Australia New Zealand Army Corps. It is celebrated at dawn, or as the Kiwis say, in another colorful colloquialism, "at the sparrow's fart." Originally, ANZAC Day had been created to celebrate the Australian and New Zealand forces that had landed on the Gallipoli Peninsula in 1915, during World War I, in an attempt to secure a sea route by which to aid Allied forces against the Ottoman Empire. The Gallipoli campaign is typically considered the beginning of Australian and New Zealand national consciousness, as it was the first time that Australian and New Zealand soldiers had fought in an international conflict under their own flags. ANZAC Day takes place on the anniversary of the landing and memorializes that portion of the more than eighteen thousand New Zealand soldiers who died in the First World War and were buried in foreign lands. Even the smallest towns have ceremonies, often with lists of the fallen, which can be long and seem entirely out of proportion to the size of the settlement. The losses were seared into the hearts and minds of all in New Zealand.

On the day itself, I answered the phone early in the morning to John and Reena inviting us to join them for a daybreak service at a memorial in Feilding. We would meet at the clock tower in the town's central square. I told John we'd be glad to go and woke Bonny.

Over time, ANZAC Day celebrations have grown to include the commemoration of all military casualties suffered by Australia and New Zealand. At this service, two young children came forward to lay a wreath in honor of their father, who had died in Afghanistan. Then members of all branches of the military marched in time to a band from Feilding, followed by a parade of war veterans, including those from a Māori battalion. A high school student from Feilding gave a speech while wearing the medals earned by her grandfather, who had fought in World War II. Finally, a lone bugler played "The Last Post" and members of the New Zealand Army performed a twenty-one-gun salute.

After everyone joined in singing the national anthem, the band played while spectators marched down the street. Bonny and I found it a moving ceremony of remembrance and unity. It was heartwarming to see a whole town come together to commemorate the fallen. New Zealand's residents enjoy a warmth and depth of community I had not known while living in the United States. I realized we were living in a country that was free of the constant friction and extreme polarization often seen in the US.

It was also simply a beautiful place, and given that I had weekends off for the first time in years, we made certain to enjoy our surroundings. The following weekend, for our first trip in New Zealand, I asked Bonny, "What do you want to do?"

She said, "Let's go tramping," using the common word for hiking in New Zealand. We booked a room at Chateau Tongariro, a hotel located in Tongariro National Park, renowned for its mountain vistas and unique alpine flora. We arrived on a misty, cloudy, windy day and, because we could see next to nothing, wondered what all the fuss was about. The next day, however, we awoke to a brilliant blue sky with the sun rising over a conical volcano known as Mount Ngauruhoe. We put on warm clothes and ventured outside to discover that we also had an amazing view of the snow-covered towering peak of Mount Ruapehu. We packed our lunch and set off for Taranaki Falls, hiking along a roaring stream where the early-morning warmth of the sun alternated with cool shadows from the branches of trees that lined the path. "Forest bathing"—soaking in the atmosphere of a forest—is my favorite activity, so I was in heaven. I was falling in love with New Zealand, and felt the place was benefiting my own spiritual well-being in all kinds of ways.

Chapter Five

BRANCHING OUT

It was illuminating to no longer be looking at the rest of the globe from within the American sociological framework, and I kept learning new things by being abroad. Both the cultural and professional experiences I had in New Zealand and in Australia were expanding my way of seeing the world, and I felt enlightened by being able to look at life from a new vantage point. In 2013, we traveled to Sydney, Australia for a three-day weekend, as I had Monday off for the Queen's birthday. We arrived on Friday night,

Bonny at Vivid Sydney

June 14th, only to be immersed in an explosion of light and music. I was amazed by what we experienced. We had arrived during Vivid Sydney, an immersive light installation with colorful projections onto the Sydney Opera House and the nearby Custom

House, combined with synchronized music. There were live performances by local and international musicians as well as lectures from leading global creative thinkers.

One inspiring lecture was from photojournalist David Burnett, who described the challenges of developing film in a hostile country like Iran. He told us the story of a now-famous black-and-white photo of the Ayatollah Khomeini that he took during the Iranian revolution. He had to take the undeveloped film to the airport and give it to strangers who were flying back to the United States, with no choice but to trust that they would get his negatives to his publisher to be developed. Out of all the film he gave to strangers at the airport, he only lost one roll.

He also witnessed the moment when the Vietnamese-American photojournalist Nick Ut captured the iconic war photograph of the "Napalm Girl" who ran screaming from her village, naked and with outstretched arms, after a bombing by an American warplane during the Vietnam War. Burnett described how Ut—who ultimately won the Pulitzer Prize for the picture—wrapped the little girl in a blanket and carried her to receive medical attention, another example of a humanitarian at work within his chosen profession.

In 2013, both Australia and New Zealand were accepting refugees from Afghanistan in large numbers, due to the war there that the United States had initiated. Many members of Afghanistan's Hazara ethnic group had served as English translators for the New Zealand Army (an ally of the US military) in Bamiyan, a city in central Afghanistan. Bonny and I began working with Red Cross refugee services to help some of the newly arrived Hazara families resettle in our area of the North Island. They arrived one afternoon by bus from Auckland, and were honored in a ceremony at Linton Army base. The eleven translators from Afghanistan were the first civilians to be awarded the New Zealand Service Medal.

When we met the particular family we were sponsoring as they got off the bus from Auckland, Naim, the head of the family, asked me, "How big is the Afghan community here?"

I said, "Well, you are it." He replied, "Oh no, I've got another migraine."

The next day, another volunteer and I took Naim shopping. After three hours of shopping and talking with other newly arrived Afghan families, we finally checked out at the Pak 'N Save. When we got back to his house, Naim said, "Which way is Mecca? I have to pray." I had no idea, but he quickly figured out which direction was northwest and knelt down to pray. The following week, we helped the family open a bank account, enroll in English classes, get approval to work, purchase a refrigerator and a washing machine, find a doctor for their three children, and get the kids enrolled in school.

In preparing for the arrival of Naim and his family, we had helped furnish their home with donated furniture. We were especially proud of the table and chairs we got for their dining room. The house was an old drafty structure with a wood stove in the living room as the only source of heat, and they had arrived in June, right in the middle of New Zealand's winter, so it was quite cold at night. Not long after they moved in, Bonny and I went for a visit and saw that all the furniture was gone. The family was sitting on the floor on rugs and pillows in front of the wood stove. When we asked what had happened to the table and chairs, they explained that they had chopped it up and burned it in the wood stove. I learned then that, in Afghan culture, it is traditional to eat and sleep on the floor, but also realized how uncomfortable they must have been. I couldn't imagine how hard it was for the families to assimilate into such a foreign place. When Bonny and I had first arrived in New Zealand, we found ourselves surrounded by a culture that had also been strongly influenced by European traditions and beliefs, so the transition had been much easier for us.

One of the newly arrived families bought their first car from a used-car-parts salvage business in Palmerston North. One day that summer, with the sun shining bright and a cool wind blowing in from the south, several of the Afghan families decided to go for a picnic on the bank of the Manawatu River. They drove the car down to the riverbank, spread out a rug, and enjoyed a flavorful Afghan meal while watching the river flow by. One of the men, who used to wash his horses in the river in Bamiyan Province, decided the car was dirty and needed a good wash. He got up from the picnic and proceeded to drive the car into the river for a proper cleaning. This shorted out all the electronics in the car and he ended up with a clean car that wouldn't start. Eventually, we were able to get a tow service to get the car out of the river. From that moment on, the episode was jokingly referred to as "the Afghan car wash."

Naim and his family ultimately decided to move to Auckland, where there was a larger Afghan community, so that they would feel less isolated culturally. We were sorry to see them go but understood completely why the decision made sense. They would have far more support in their new location.

Meanwhile, at the hospital, I kept learning new things about other cultures as well. When I arrived, the hospital had doctors from South Africa and Malaysia, as well as another American. Physicians from Iceland and Great Britain would later join our team. My closest friends and colleagues were almost all from countries other than the United States. In terms of how to treat our patients respectfully, however, I learned the most valuable lessons from the registrar and the head nurse, both of whom were Māori. They had explained to me, for example, why so many family members had to be present when a loved one died—that unless this were the case, according to Māori culture, the person who passed would have to journey to the next world all alone. I also had a habit of occasionally taking a seat on countertops or tables during rounds, as otherwise I would be spending the entire day on my feet. Little did I know that sitting on a table is taboo in Māori culture. Thankfully, the head nurse clued me in to this mistake, and I was able to rectify my behavior. He and the registrar also taught me a few basic Māori phrases so that I could greet patients in their own home language, such as *haere mai* and *kia ora*. When I spoke these words to Māori patients, I could see their expressions brighten. I would also use the Māori word for family, *whānau*. Expressing even basic greetings in Māori made a huge impact on my ability to build trust with my patients.

Another important lesson that my new colleagues shared with me was the idea that work and life could be balanced in a healthy way, even for those in the health professions. This had not been the case in the United States, where it was considered imperative for doctors to work an extraordinary number of hours in order to be viewed as team players by their colleagues. While I worked in Florida, I had tried to take a month off every summer so that I could spend time with my family. We would take a big trip of some kind and strengthen our family ties. My colleagues were angered by this, however, and they let me know. They viewed my absence as a burden for them, because when I left, they had to handle my nights and weekends on call, adding to their own levels of stress. I thought it was important for me to have strong relationships with my wife and my children, and I wished the other cardiologists would adopt the same kind of vacation schedules themselves so that we could take turns being away, but the idea was considered anathema by my American colleagues.

Not so in New Zealand. I still worked long hours by normal standards, but I was on call far less often. In the US, when I was working as an interventional cardiologist, I had been on call every third evening, meaning that I had to be at the hospital within an hour if a patient had a heart attack, ready to open up a blocked artery. Often, this would happen at night. I remember one instance vividly, as the case took an unexpected turn. I got the call at about 2 a.m. A woman had suffered a heart attack while in the emergency room of the local hospital in Florida. She had an ST-segment elevation myocardial infarction, which means that one of the main arteries that supply the heart with blood had been blocked abruptly. Because we suspected a clot was blocking the coronary artery, other members of the team had given her blood-thinning medication before I arrived, an essential step in preparing her for the procedure I was to perform. What I did not know when I began the procedure was that she had been feeling very sick to her stomach and had vomited during the heart attack. Thinking she still had the blood-thinning medication Plavix in her system, I took the patient into the cath lab, where I immediately opened the coronary artery and put in a stent, and her condition stabilized shortly thereafter. Then she was taken to the ICU for recovery and observation, and it was there that everything suddenly went awry. She experienced a return of her chest pain, then exhibited ST elevation all over again. I could not understand why this would be the case and reached out to other members of the team to review what had happened. Had they given her the blood-thinning medication? Yes, they had, I was told—but then she had thrown up. As soon as I heard that she had been sick to her stomach, I knew that she had almost certainly vomited up the medication before it could take effect. Quite likely, her body had formed another clot.

We took the patient back up to the cath lab, re-administered the blood thinning medication, and reopened the same coronary artery all over again. Indeed, her body had formed a clot around the metal stent, blocking the capacity for blood to flow through the device. Thankfully, we were able to clean out the new blockage and restore blood flow to the heart once more, and this time the patient stayed stable in the ICU. By that point it was about 5 a.m., almost time for rounds to begin. I was exhausted, but you did not get the day off simply because you had been on call the night before. I simply went back to work.

Of course, this kind of punishing schedule takes a toll on physicians, but at that point in my career I viewed it as normal. Later I would come to appreciate more fully how detrimental this lifestyle can be. A national survey published in the *Archives of Internal Medicine* in 2012 reported that US physicians suffer more burnout than most other American workers. About 45.8 percent of physicians were experiencing at least one symptom of burnout, according to the study: loss of enthusiasm for work, feelings of cynicism, or a low sense of personal accomplishment. When cardiologists were given the same criteria, 38 percent responded they felt burned out, while 49.5 percent cited being under stress and having less energy, according to the June 2019 American College of Cardiology's third Professional Life Survey.

And so it was with a sense of gratitude that I began to enjoy having weekends and nights off more regularly, for the first time in my professional life. Once I began working in New Zealand, I was only on call for five consecutive weeknights every three or four weeks, whereas my American colleagues were on call many more weeknights and on weekends as well. I took full advantage of this incredible perk to explore our new surroundings, and Bonny and I traveled as much as we could to take in the natural splendor of New Zealand.

In June 2013, for our twenty-ninth wedding anniversary, Bonny and I headed off for a romantic weekend at a hunting lodge in Rotorua, on the North Island, that some friends in Florida had recommended. When we arrived at the Treetop Lodge, we encountered for the first time the famous silver fern, the national symbol of New Zealand. The underside of the fern is silver, and the Māori have historically used the plant to mark their paths at night, as the leaves shimmer in the moonlight. At the lodge, we were greeted with a picnic lunch and were given directions to Bridal Veil Falls, where water cascades over a rock formation and spreads out in a fine spray like a veil. On the way back, we did not get lost because we had marked our trail with silver ferns, laying down the leaves glistening-side up, according to the tradition.

Along the trail near the entrance to the lodge, we were greeted by a stone carving of a Māori god. Bonny went for a horseback ride, while I tried my hand at pheasant hunting. First, a guide took me out and showed me how to lead the clay pigeons with a shotgun. I then tried leading a living target as my guide's pointers flushed the birds out from under the bushes into the air. I was able to bag the first three birds that the dogs flushed out.

Feeling a sense of accomplishment, I brought the birds to the lodge's walk-in fridge to hang for aging. Then it was off for a drink in the hot tub with Bonny. She told me that her guide had been a Māori man who was eighty-six years old and very connected with his natural surroundings. He had shared with her the names of the plants and birds they encountered on their ride; she was especially impressed with the cabbage tree, which grows up to sixty feet tall and produces a fruit that is a favorite food source for the *kererū*, a native bird.

The guide had also told her about his spiritual home, the *marae*, a meeting ground with a long wood building used for family gatherings and funerals. As of 2020, there are nearly eight hundred *marae* across New Zealand, sacred places at the living heart of Māori culture and society.

I had begun snow-skiing when I was a fourteen-year-old freshman in high school, when I learned the sport on a rope-tow hill called Bell Mountain in Mercer County, New Jersey. Since that time, I had dreamed of going heli-skiing in fresh untracked powder. In July 2013, winter in New Zealand, I got the opportunity to do so, and learned another essential aspect of the local culture in the process.

My youngest son Jeffery, my mother Gloria, Bonny, and I flew down to Queenstown on the South Island for a ski holiday. We stayed at Blanket Bay on beautiful Lake Wakatipu. The lodge booked us a trip up the mountain with a heli-ski company for Sunday. The day dawned bright and clear, and we awoke with the excitement of a new adventure but also some anxiety about the danger of steep slopes and deep snow. We had warmed up the day before at a ski resort just outside of Queenstown, however, so we felt prepared for the challenge.

We arrived at the heliport on Lake Wanaka for a safety briefing with our guides. We received avalanche beacons in case we found ourselves buried in ten or more feet of snow, and learned how to do the "chopper huddle," which involves huddling together and keeping a hand on your guide's pack when the helicopter both lifts off and swoops down to pick you up.

We then loaded our skis and snowboards onto the helicopter and flew up the mountain to our drop-off point. We landed on a tiny ledge about eight thousand feet above the valley floor. We did the chopper huddle and the helicopter lifted off as the downdraft whipped up snow all around us. As I put on my skis, I looked over the edge to the valley floor, an intimidating distance below.

Our guide Chris made it clear that we needed to follow his path assiduously, so that we wouldn't ski off a cliff by mistake. This sounded like good advice. Then it was off down the mountain for some fresh powder skiing. At one point, I skied a little bit too close to a precipice, looked over the edge, and saw a terrifying chasm. This was alarming, and I felt a jolt of fear. I called out to Chris and asked him to

Heli-skiing with Jeffery

indicate the best way down. He answered with a classic New Zealand response: "No worries, mate! Just follow me. I'll show you the way."

After the first run, our fear and anxiety evaporated in the sheer exhilaration of carving through untracked powder. We had a wonderful day of heli-skiing and completed four runs. At one point I did ski off a cliff; thankfully, the drop was moderate, and I landed safely. Then, on our last run, I went right, and the rest of the group went left. I soon found myself at the edge of a very steep rock face, this time looking down on the valley below. There was no safe route down from where I was, and I had no choice but to make a thirty-minute climb back up the mountain and over a nearby ridge, so I could ski down to the group. As the helicopter came to pick us up after our last run, we felt a sense of accomplishment and relief that everyone had ended the day safely.

The next month, I arranged to go to the Cardiac Society of Australia and New Zealand's annual meeting on the Gold Coast of Australia. Our daughter Kirsten joined me, my mother, Bonny, and Jeffery for an adventure on the Great Barrier Reef. We flew into Lizard Island, off the northeast coast of Australia. This part of Australia is near the equator, and the climate is quite tropical—even in the month of August, when it is technically winter. Kirsten, Jeffery, and I took a refresher course so we could go diving on the Great Barrier Reef. The next morning, we prepared to go diving at the famous Cod Hole.

Descending through the warm blue water, we encountered giant potato cod, huge greyish-brown fish with black polka dots that will swim right up to you. These impressive cod can grow to be six feet long and weigh up to 240 pounds. We also saw giant clams, an endangered species protected from being harvested that can reach up to four feet across and weigh up to five hundred pounds. Between heli-skiing in the Southern Alps of New Zealand and diving at the Great Barrier Reef of Australia, it had been quite a couple of months, and I felt incredibly fortunate to have had the opportunity to see more of this part of the world. After each of these adventures, immersed in the healing power of time amidst natural beauty, I also felt more ready to return to work, refreshed and rejuvenated in a way that I had rarely felt while working in the United States. My time in New Zealand was restoring a lost balance to my professional life, and I was sure that, if other doctors could experience that balance as well, it would help mitigate the enormous stress physicians experience in hospital wards where they work so intensely to save the lives of others. Instead of burning out, I was branching out, and if I had been given the power to do so, I would have written a prescription for every cardiologist in the United States to take at least two whole days off each week, to spend more time with their families and more time outside in nature.

Chapter Six

OUTSIDE THE COMFORT ZONE

Practicing medicine in New Zealand required me to get out of my comfort zone and learn how to perform new techniques. Despite my age of sixty-two, I still had an open mind and a willingness to learn, and this was critical to my future success. I had a belief that my abilities were not fixed but could continue to improve.

The technique called transesophageal echocardiography involves the insertion of a long thin tube—an endoscope—down the esophagus in order to guide an ultrasound probe, which can then take pictures of the heart without the ribs or lungs getting in the way. Transesophageal echo is a way to get a better look at the heart and rule out clots or heart valve infection, called endocarditis. It is considered a diagnostic gold standard in New Zealand, and all cardiologists practicing there are required to learn it. In all my years of working in the United States, I had never been trained to perform this procedure, simply because it was introduced after I finished my cardiology fellowship training.

When I began looking for training opportunities in transesophageal echo before we moved to New Zealand, the only ones I could find were for anesthesiologists, because they often use this technique to monitor the heart during surgery on that organ. I found two clinical preceptorships, one at Duke University Medical Center and the other at the University of Nebraska Medical Center. Duke had an excellent reputation, and at Nebraska they offered an online skills review after you completed the program. I signed up for and completed both courses, then began to look for a place where I could do the hands-on practical training. It became clear that cardiology programs did not want to train anyone in transesophageal echo other than their own cardiology fellows, which was understandable. I finally found an opportunity to perform transesophageal echocardiograms at Memorial Hospital in Jacksonville, Florida, where I had previously been on call covering weekends with another group of doctors. My Memorial cardiology colleagues helped me complete forty of these procedures. Then I was ready to go to New Zealand.

I had not been working in New Zealand for long when my training was put to the test. I received a referral from one of my colleagues to perform a transesophageal echo in order to evaluate the progression of the patient's valvular heart disease. I pulled up the patient's chart and discovered he had an esophageal pouch, or diverticulum, coming off of his esophagus. If the echo probe went down the pouch instead of the esophagus, it could lead to rupture of the esophagus and death. Since an echo probe is placed without direct visualization of the esophagus, a transesophageal echo was absolutely contraindicated and risky in this patient. Lesson learned: do a complete chart review, looking for any contraindications, before performing a transesophageal echo.

Another essential skill I learned was how to put a needle through the chest wall into the heart lining to drain fluid from around the heart, a procedure called pericardiocentesis. One night, I was called in for an emergency at about 2 a.m., and when I answered the phone I heard the tense, anxious voice of an intensive care physician asking me to perform an emergency heart echocardiogram on a patient who had just undergone surgery. He was having an inferior-wall heart attack with low blood pressure, which the intensive care physician was unable to raise. I arrived with an echo machine and saw the patient in a corner bed in the intensive care unit. Clear plastic bags containing medicated fluids were hanging from a metal pole near his bed, hooked up to multiple infusion pumps that flashed like Christmas lights. The echo we performed at bedside showed normal cardiovascular function but a moderate amount of fluid around the heart, the pressure of which was causing blood to back up after each heart contraction, a condition called cardiac tamponade.

While performing the echo, I suddenly sensed someone behind me, and when I turned to look through darkness, there stood a physician in scrubs with the image from my own monitor reflecting off his glasses. His face wasn't entirely clear, but I gathered he was the surgeon who had performed the initial operation. I asked him if he had gone anywhere near the heart during the surgery. "I put surgical staples through the diaphragm to tack up the esophagus," he responded.

Knowing the inferior wall of the heart rests on the other side of the diaphragm, I instantly understood why the heart tracings and blood tests looked like an inferior-wall heart attack. Right away, I contacted Wellington, our referral center for open-heart surgery. My colleague there advised us to perform pericardiocentesis—to put a needle in the fluid around the heart and drain it—and said they would transfer the patient in the morning. I had never before performed a successful pericardiocentesis procedure, and believed that even if the procedure were performed perfectly, the blood would just reaccumulate and the patient would not be around in the morning. Much to my relief, I prevailed in sending him to Wellington by life flight. My colleague performed a coronary angiogram, which showed no damage to the arteries supplying blood to the heart. He then tried to drain the blood from around the heart with a needle, only for it to reaccumulate, as I had anticipated. The patient subsequently went into cardiac arrest and was taken to the operating theater with my colleague sitting beside him on the stretcher, frantically draining blood into a tube to prevent it from reaccumulating in the pericardium, the tissue membrane that surrounds the heart.

The cardiovascular surgeons opened the patient's chest and found staples through the diaphragm into the heart, causing bleeding from the cardiac veins. The bleeding was stopped with repair of the cardiac veins, and the patient made a complete recovery. I felt quite chuffed at this outcome, a term my Kiwi colleagues used to describe beaming with pride. Take-home message: I needed to learn how to drain fluid from around the heart so I could save someone's life in an emergency, and more importantly, one should never try to drain a traumatic pericardial effusion without a cardiovascular surgeon present.

Since moving to New Zealand, I had been impressed by the sheer number of these cardiac tamponades—the term for the compression of the heart due to an accumulation of fluid in the pericardial sac—that required emergency pericardiocentesis. While in the United States, I had only been taught the posterior approach to draining pericardial fluid, rather than the anterior approach, which is actually much easier and therefore better suited to emergencies. This latter approach to pericardiocentesis, therefore, was an essential skill that I needed to master. After the case of the patient I sent to Wellington, my colleagues taught me how to access the pericardium by coming in from a point just to the left of the sternum, and to my immense gratification I was able to successfully drain accumulated fluid from several patients using this procedure, bringing them immediate relief.

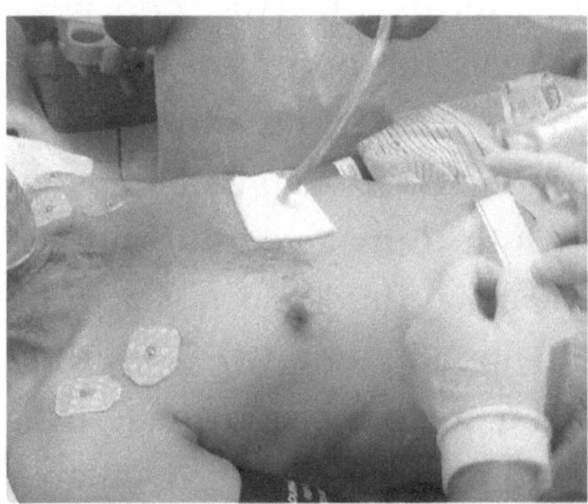

One morning after rounds, I was called to see an anxious middle-aged man from Nepal who presented with breathlessness, an enlarged heart, a mass in his left upper lung, and left pleural effusion, or fluid around his left lung. On exam, I could see that the patient was indeed short of breath and that he had low blood pressure. His systolic blood pressure—the force the heart exerts when it beats—was only 90 mm, and he had a pulsus paradoxus of 15-20 mm Hg, meaning we could detect a fall in blood pressure each time he inhaled. We therefore suspected tamponade, or compression of the heart. The patient underwent an urgent echocardiogram, which showed a large pericardial effusion with collapse of the right ventricle in diastole—the period of time when the heart is relaxed and filling with blood—a confirmation of tamponade.

The patient was taken to the procedure room and elevated from a supine position to a seated one to ease his breathing. We performed another echo and could see a clear path to the fluid around his heart from the fifth intercostal space between the ribs, demonstrating an acceptable location for pericardiocentesis. The area was sterilized with antiseptic cleaning fluid and sterile drape applied. We administered local anesthesia with lidocaine, and I inserted a pericardiocentesis needle anteriorly into the fluid, after confirming via ultrasound that this was the optimum location. While continuously pulling back on the syringe, I withdrew pale, bloody fluid. The syringe was disconnected from the needle and the liquid was dripped on a white cloth to make sure it did not clot, confirming it was indeed pericardial fluid and not arterial blood from inside the heart. A soft-tipped guide wire was then inserted, the needle withdrawn, and a small incision made over the entry site, permitting us to insert a dilator catheter to enlarge the pathway to the fluid around the heart. A device called a multiple side-hole pigtail catheter was then inserted, and the guide wire removed. We were then able to use multiple 20-cc syringes to withdraw over a liter of bloody pericardial fluid.

While samples of the pericardial fluid were sent to the lab for analysis, we saw a marked improvement in the patient's blood pressure, and a repeat echo confirmed nearly complete resolution of the pericardial effusion. The pigtail catheter was sutured in place and connected to a negative-pressure vacuum; it was important to leave the drain in place until the drainage of fluid from the pericardium stopped. The pericardial sac has roughly a two-liter capacity, so after you drain more than two liters of pericardial fluid, you should be less concerned about further accumulation. When the pericardium is empty, the patient will start to develop discomfort from the pericardial drainage tube, and it is safe to remove the tube.

In this instance, we removed the drainage tube after two days, and the patient became completely asymptomatic and was able to walk out of the hospital three days later. Our analysis of the pericardial fluid unfortunately returned a cytology test that was positive for adenocarcinoma, a lethal type of cancer, meaning that the patient probably did not have long to live. Still, we hoped that we had given him at least a few more weeks or months of time with his family back in Nepal. Draining fluid from around the heart in a patient with tamponade is a gratifying experience, because you take a patient who is in extreme distress and turn that person into someone who is smiling in relief from the resolution of suffering.

———————

I also re-familiarized myself with all the minor tasks I had rarely done on a routine basis in the States, from applying bandages to removing IVs. In Florida, I had been the co-director of nuclear cardiology at my hospital. This meant that I helped design medical protocols which were followed by nurses, nuclear techs, and cardiology techs. They were the ones who injected the patients, stressed the patients, administered basic tests, and did just about everything else. Working in New Zealand, however, I learned that doctors there often did many of the small tasks that American doctors might consider beneath them. Culturally, New Zealand is the home of DIY, and in their off-hours my colleagues could often be found fixing up their own homes, rather than hiring other people to do that labor.

Soon I, too, became a one-man band, and found that I appreciated the humility involved in practicing medicine this way. When doing a nuclear stress test, for example, I would get the sestamibi, a radioactive heart-tracer material, from the nuclear technologist in the hot lab. Then I would mix the stress agent adenosine, record the dose, and infuse it intravenously to chemically stress the heart. I would inject the sestamibi in order to light up the heart on the scan, then remove the IV, bandage the puncture site, and call transport to move the patient to the nuclear medicine lab, where the heart would be scanned by the nuclear technologist. And at the end of the day, I would read the heart scan and call the referring physician to arrange follow-up if needed, before turning out the reading room lights. In performing all of these tasks myself, I learned to appreciate all that is involved in obtaining a quality study. If

the radioactive injection was done poorly or the chemical stress agent was not correctly administered, one could skew the results—and, more importantly, one could affect a patient's health.

On a deeper level, handling all these steps in the care of a given patient meant that I felt more emotionally connected to that individual, and I was also in a better position to witness the effect of the care being provided on the patient's well-being. Back in the United States, the provision of care had grown so fragmented that often entirely different medical experts would handle each step of the care process, and those different parties did not always communicate perfectly. Because hospitals in New Zealand had more limited resources, physicians handled more aspects of a patient's care themselves. Thus I was able to regain a degree of control over individual patient care that I felt had been lost in the American medical system. Having one central person involved in the majority of decisions meant there were fewer gaps in communication, and the care we provided was therefore more consistent. In essence, I felt able to return to the way I had practiced medicine at an earlier point in my career, before the hyper-focus on sub-specialties caused fragmentation of caregiving and a loss of sensitivity toward the patient as a human being. By becoming more of a generalist again, I felt more in control of how care was administered to my patients, and the caregiving that my team and I provided felt more holistic.

In New Zealand, there were 20 local district health boards responsible for providing or funding health services in their communities. These boards divided healthcare resources to allow equal access to all members of their respective communities. Since 2001, the key focus has been on strengthening primary care services that can be provided closer to home, in community settings, and with a stronger emphasis on disease prevention. For instance, there is limited access to cardiac surgery, with only five hospitals providing publicly funded cardiac surgery in all of New Zealand. That translates to roughly one hospital for every million people in the country. By comparison, in the United States, there are over 1,000 hospitals that offer cardiac surgery—one hospital for every 33,000 people—and they provide 500,000 invasive valve replacement and coronary bypass surgeries every year.

———————

Back in America, I had tended to go through my life at full speed yet had always stayed within the realm of what I already knew, and so I didn't generally learn new techniques as a physician or grow as a person. I had always been in a hurry because of the urgency of treating patients in dire circumstances and the pressure of the American hospital system to treat as many patients as possible, so much so that I didn't take the time to relate much to my colleagues and only developed a few close professional relationships. In New Zealand, where I finally had the bandwidth to slow down and reflect, I began changing those habits. I became very close with a colleague from Iceland, Darri Karlsson, who was very kind. He and his wife Tora would invite me over for dinner when Bonny was back in the United States, and we spent many delightful evenings talking about our life experiences.

Another colleague with whom I developed a close professional relationship was Nathan Better, a good-natured cardiologist from Melbourne. I had invited Nathan to help set up our nuclear cardiology lab at the hospital in New Zealand because of his expertise in that realm. He recommended that the lab start reporting the calcium build-up in the coronary arteries, which we could see visually on CT scans of the heart. We started to include quantitative visual calcium scores in our nuclear heart scan reports, and so began our research into coronary calcium—an endeavor that would ultimately change my career and, in part, the field of cardiology itself. Nathan also turned out to be a delightful human being who knew all the rules of Aussie football and was crazy about his home team, the Carlton Blues. He enjoyed traveling to unusual places, as did I, and we became close, traveling with our wives together to the Atacama Desert in Chile, among other destinations.

In all these ways, the years I spent in New Zealand challenged me professionally and personally. It was here that I realized the acquisition of wisdom begins at the end of one's comfort zone. There were times when I felt uncomfortable, but I kept an open mind, and those experiences ultimately helped me grow as a person. I even had the opportunity to learn to paraglide with my daughter Kirsten in 2014, when she visited while on a break before starting her master's degree. I felt pure exhilaration while gliding through a brilliant blue sky, flying high above the emerald lake known as Wakatipu. "Come to New Zealand and we will take you to jump off a mountain," I declared in a blog post about our experience. Later, one of my former colleagues from the clinic came to visit, and he and his wife and I did just that. I had been changed by moving to New Zealand, and I was overjoyed to be able to share that new way of being in the world with others.

Chapter Seven

JUDDER BAR FLUTTER

In January 2014, at the height of summer in New Zealand, Bonny and I moved to a rented country house just outside of Feilding, where we could kick off our shoes and wiggle our toes in the soft grass. We were in the countryside getting back in touch with nature, and we found enormous pleasure in doing so. The house was in the middle of some of the most beautiful countryside in New Zealand, and we were surrounded by rolling green hills covered with grazing sheep. We had our own garden from which we harvested lots of fresh vegetables. We even acquired two sheep after they wandered into our yard and started eating the flowers. We asked around regarding their owner, but no one claimed them, so we herded them into a fenced-in field next to the house. Our landlord's father owned a flock of sheep himself. One touching experience was seeing the flock's orphaned lambs being bottle-fed by the small children of the community. It was a warm feeling, seeing five- and six-year-old boys and girls nurturing the lambs, who would come running to suck eagerly on the bottles.

There were lots of birds in the country. Small fantails, which expand and then flutter their tail feathers in order to float above the ground, flew around the small stream that ran through the property. So did tui, black birds with distinctive throat tufts of curled white feathers. The tui has a staccato call with a constantly changing pitch, and we heard it all around us. The area was also home to many brown rabbits, and harrier hawks with their majestic wingspans circled above, looking for a meal. The fields were filled with barley and corn, and flowers bloomed everywhere. We were walking in the paddock one day, and some young bulls started toward us, so I reached my hands high above my head and made a loud noise. They stopped in their tracks, and we made sure to stay out of that field in the future. Otherwise, our time in the countryside was mostly calming, and we enjoyed feeling the ebb and flow of the natural environment around us. One of the most spectacular things about living in the countryside was the clear night sky, full of brightly twinkling stars. The Milky Way jumped right out at us, and we felt an exhilarating sense of wonder at the vastness of the universe.

The natural world surprised us in an entirely new fashion one afternoon, when we saw the kitchen ceiling light start to sway back and forth. Soon it felt like the floor was rolling, and then the dishes started to rattle. I shouted to Bonny, "We need to get outside!" We ran out into the backyard, where we felt the ground moving under our feet. Fortunately, the earthquake stopped after about a minute, but while it was happening, it was scary. Our home suffered minimal damage, just a few broken dishes, but it was an unnerving experience. Seismic events would occur several times while we lived in New Zealand, but we were never again as blindsided as we had been by that first earthquake.

Meanwhile, I spent time providing care to the community in Levin, a town in a rural part of the North Island. One day each week—as long as I was not on call—I worked in an outreach clinic that provided medical services to an underserved population there. In the United States, rural communities had been devastated by the changes in healthcare, as revenue-oriented health organizations closed hundreds of small community hospitals and clinics that once served rural populations. Those clinics and community hospitals had lost money or had made less money than bigger hospitals located in more densely populated locations, and had been bought out or had seen their staff whisked away by corporate hospitals. The American Hospital Association reports that there were 136 rural hospital closures in the decade between 2010 and 2021 in the US. In both urban and rural areas, pediatric departments in hospitals have been vanishing, and hospitals have been prioritizing adult admissions, because they cannot make money serving children. Meanwhile, the *Wall Street Journal* reports big nonprofit hospital chains shunning poorer communities, closing hospitals and clinics in those areas, and relocating personnel and resources to their entities in wealthier regions across the US. Whether the hospitals call themselves for-profit or nonprofit has become irrelevant, as entities once run by religious or charitable organizations are now run as business propositions, however they file their tax forms. Poor areas—urban and rural—may soon be completely without services for key segments of the population. Who will care for those people?

By contrast, in New Zealand, the healthcare system has retained a strong emphasis on providing care to underserved areas, a priority that remains feasible to maintain, even though it is not lucrative, because of the public funding of healthcare. Most of the doctors I worked with traveled to one of the rural clinics located throughout the region we served one day a week. Most Tuesday mornings, I would check out a car from the hospital carpool and drive one hour south to Levin, where I would conduct an all-day cardiology clinic. Levin is a town of nineteen thousand, located about fifty kilometers southwest of Palmerston North. On a sunny morning, the drive was quite beautiful, as I would head toward the snowcapped Tararua mountain range, silhouetted against the clear blue horizon. In Levin, a nurse would sit in while I took histories and performed physical exams, which I found helpful, as the nurses usually knew the patients well. The nurses also taught patients how to manage diabetes and other chronic conditions, while echo teams conducted echocardiograms, tests which many of these patients might not have been able to access otherwise. The patients I saw in the cardiology clinic had been referred by family practitioners, and typical complaints included arrhythmia, hearts damaged by a cardiac event or adversely impacted by infection, as well as calcified heart valves. Sometimes I recommended an echocardiogram or made a referral to a larger facility for a valve replacement or a coronary angiogram. After a full day in the clinic, I would drive back and be home in time for dinner. This weekly commitment proved deeply meaningful, and I came to value the time in the field because of the service-oriented aspect of the care we provided. There was enormous joy for me in the fact that I could once again function more like a primary care physician and see the patient as a whole person, rather than being stuck in a dehumanizing routine of specialized tasks. It was the closest I came to truly practicing medicine the way I wanted to since I had owned my own practice back in the United States.

Another one of the great pleasures of working in New Zealand was getting to interact with young doctors in training. I loved the interaction between doctors during rounds, as we function much like detectives: trying to solve the reason for a given patient's illness, come up with a solid diagnosis, and formulate an appropriate treatment plan. I always enjoyed the energy and enthusiasm of the young interns fresh out of medical school with their whole lives before them. They had unlimited potential to be anything they wanted to be, and on rounds they showed a boundless and infectious enthusiasm for learning. I remember one teaching case quite vividly. A thirty-eight-year-old Māori woman presented six days after a difficult vaginal delivery with severe chest pain and shortness of breath. She had been hypertensive during pregnancy, and her delivery had been quite arduous, with a lot of straining and pushing. Yet her presentation was quite puzzling: she was too young for this to be a heart attack, even though her chest pain suggested one. The house officers and I began to play detective. In the emergency room, they performed a CT of the chest to rule out a pulmonary embolus, or a blood clot to the lung. The CT was negative for a clot, but it showed a pericardial effusion, meaning she had fluid around her heart. When I listened to her chest, I heard a heart murmur that suggested a leaking aortic valve. I then ordered an emergency echocardiogram to evaluate her aortic valve, and it showed marked dilation of the ascending aorta and a moderate leak of the aortic valve, as well as fluid around the heart. As I looked at the echocardiogram, it was as though a light came on in my head, and I had an "aha" moment. I told the house staff that I believed her chest pain was caused by an aortic dissection, or tear, and we ordered an emergency CT angiogram of the ascending aorta.

It wasn't long, however, until a breathless intern arrived from radiology to tell me that the radiologist had not seen a dissection on the CT angiogram. I motioned for the house officers to come with me, and we bounded down the stairs to the CT suite. Upon careful review with the radiologist, we realized he had somehow missed the dissection entirely, and there was indeed a tear that we defined as a type A dissection of the ascending aorta. As the two-week mortality for an untreated dissection of that kind is 75 percent, and we were on day six since the tear had most likely occurred, the patient was life-flighted to Wellington for emergency open-heart surgery. A Bentall's procedure was performed, meaning the surgeons replaced the ascending aorta and aortic valve. She did well and had a quick recovery, and a few days later she was happy to go home to be with her newborn.

While it's not common for radiologists to miss major dissections or other obvious, life-threatening abnormalities, this case demonstrated the importance of sticking with your gut response as a physician and taking responsibility to review the images that you've ordered yourself. This is especially true in cases when the radiology report is

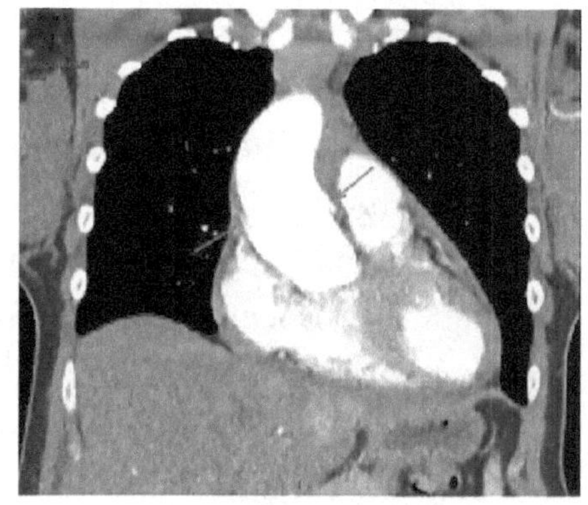

Arrows pointing to the tear
in the ascending aorta

not consistent with a patient's general presentation. For me personally, it was also an example of the collaborative possibilities that exist within medicine, and that the New Zealand healthcare system encouraged rather than diminished.

During my time in New Zealand, I was also able, with the help of our pharmacist Anthea, to initiate a program that allowed high school seniors who were trying to decide about a future career in the health care field to join us on rounds in the hospital. I remember the first student that went through the program. Matt was a high school student from Palmerston North whose parents were friends of ours, and he wasn't sure if he wanted to become a doctor. I declared one evening at dinner, "If you're not sure about being a doctor, why don't you come on rounds with me and see what it's like." Matt and his family were excited about the prospect of him seeing medicine practiced in person. I approached the cardiology administrator with the idea, which she promptly rejected. Undeterred, I then approached Anthea with the same idea, and got an enthusiastic response. So Matt made rounds with me as a visitor from the pharmacy department, paving the way for other students to have the same opportunity. It was an interesting morning with many fascinating cases, and the experience reinforced Matt's determination to become a doctor. Matt went on to complete medical school and is now an intern at the hospital and the program we helped initiate together is still alive and doing well, allowing many other young people to follow in his footsteps.

———————

One day, I was in the hospital on rounds when I was presented with the case of an elderly gentlemen with chest pain, who had reportedly experienced a life-threatening heart rhythm disturbance called ventricular fibrillation and ventricular tachycardia (VFIB/VTACH) during the ambulance ride to the hospital. The paramedic's notes said the patient's vital signs were originally stable, with a blood pressure of 136/74, until the rhythm disturbance occurred. The notes also said he looked remarkably well during the VFIB/VTACH episode. At the bedside, the patient told us that the ambulance had taken an especially rough and bumpy road to the hospital.

Looking at the rhythm strip, I noticed normal sinus rhythm followed by wide undulating complexes that then returned to sinus rhythm. The heart-tracing spikes, or QRS complexes, marched out unchanged, so I concluded that the so-called disturbance was actually caused by the ambulance going over a rough patch of road. Speed bumps in New Zealand are called judder bars, so I explained to the house staff that this was a judder bar artifact. One of my colleagues suggested I write this up and call it "judder bar flutter." In other words, the patient only needed to be treated for a mild case of chest pain, and nothing more—the paramedic had actually seen evidence of a road in need of repair, not an actual case of an abnormal heart rhythm, on the ambulance's monitor.

Then one of my colleagues told me another story of "judder bar flutter" that is not so funny. A young lady with chest pain phoned the community rescue unit, and the two responders decided to transport her to our hospital. She was placed in the back of the ambulance with a new trainee and hooked up to a monitor that had the ability to defibrillate, while the more experienced responder drove the ambulance. While going over a rough patch of road, the monitor's alarm went off, and its automated voice blared out: "Shock advised." Just as the trainee reached for the flashing orange shock button, the veteran, seeing that the patient was sitting up and in no distress, realized this was another instance of "judder bar flutter" and shouted out, "Don't shock the patient!" But it was too late: the flashing orange button had already been pressed, and the patient had been shocked. The veteran quickly pulled over, told the trainee to get up front and drive, and said he would stay in the back with the patient. In the hospital, the patient expressed her surprise about being shocked. "I don't know why they shocked me; I was feeling fine!" she exclaimed, according to one of our nurses. That nurse often used the term gobsmacked, and I thought this exactly described how that patient must have felt when she was defibrillated out of the blue. The moral of this story is simple: don't shock an alert patient with stable vital signs when there is a lot of unusual motion in the emergency vehicle, as it may be that the road itself has caused a heart rhythm artifact.

While practicing medicine in New Zealand remained overall a positive experience, I also recall spells of difficulty at work due to the high turnover rate among the doctors on our staff. While many expat physicians who moved to New Zealand responded with the same kind of enthusiasm as I did, some found the working conditions challenging compared with what they were used to, particularly the grunt work that we were expected to do in the hospital. When they left, we were rendered short-handed. At various intervals, the number of cardiologists in our hospital dropped down to only two or three, and then we would all work longer hours and be on call more frequently until we could recruit additional team members. At one point, a colleague who had been in charge of the department left for another hospital, and afterwards I served as interim director of the cardiology unit for several months. The administration then appointed a different colleague to the role in a permanent capacity. His appointment sparked controversy in the hospital and the community at large, because previously he had been accused of being involved in a drunken attack on his partner, for which he narrowly escaped an assault conviction.

At the same time, this doctor was highly intelligent and clinically competent. He was from another country but knew our community well, as he had practiced in the district as an internist before going to Wellington for specialist training in cardiology. Like many of us, he had taken refuge from his home country's healthcare system in New Zealand—a place of unusual tolerance, where hospital administrators were sometimes willing to look past even serious past behavioral issues as long as the reformed doctor served his patients and the institution well. This physician proved helpful at reducing a backlog of referral cases and streamlining our overall efficiency, and the administration viewed him in a positive light. At the same time, many of us found his manner overbearing, and we were relieved when he left the hospital about one year later.

After his departure, nobody wanted to serve as head of the department, which involved wading through a large amount of additional paperwork. The hospital allowed the position to remain vacant, and I soon found myself enjoying an even greater degree of autonomy. This also allowed me to pursue my research interest in coronary calcium, a topic that I would investigate more fully and write about in the years that followed. Only by working in New Zealand, where I was given time to pursue original research and where I had the chance to work in a medical system that prioritized conservation of limited resources, was I able to contribute to insights that would help change the field of cardiology.

Chapter Eight

LEGACY

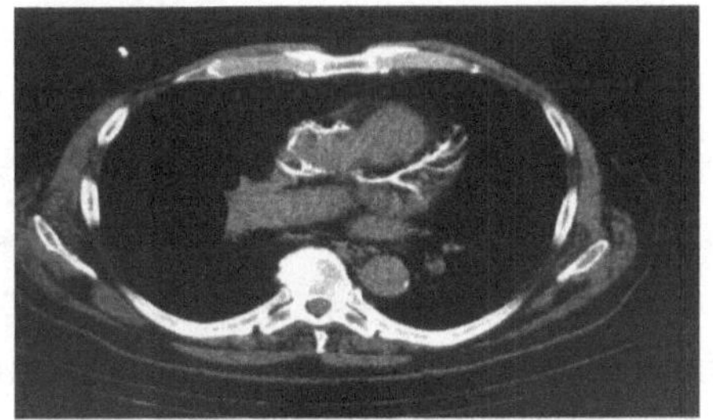

CT attenuation image demonstrating severe
calcification of the coronary arteries

When my colleague from Melbourne, Nathan Better, arrived to help set up our nuclear cardiology lab, we were typically obtaining a CT attenuation correction chest scan and a myocardial blood flow study for all patients, but we were reporting only the results of the blood flow studies to the doctors who had referred those patients to us. During a coronary blood flow study, a camera records the heart muscle's uptake of radioactive heart tracers, and under stress the blood flow study will show the severity of cholesterol blockage in the coronary artery. In blood flow studies, the greater the uptake of the radioactive tracer by the heart, the greater the blood flow, and the brighter the image. The more severe the blockage, the less the heart muscle will take up the tracer during stress.

A computed tomography scan, commonly called a CT scan, is a computer-generated x-ray of the heart with especially high resolution. The CT scans demonstrated how much of that brightness might be diminished by the soft tissue in the chest, such as a woman's breast, allowing us to adjust our reading of the blood flow studies accordingly. The CTs also happened to indicate the amount of calcium buildup in the coronary artery, but this was never reported, as it was secondary to the main purpose of the attenuation correction scan. When Nathan arrived, he suggested that we also report the coronary calcium buildup visible on the attenuation correction CT scans. Because the CT scans show high resolution images, they can detect calcium often not visible on an ordinary x-ray of the chest. Calcium appears as a bright area on a heart CT image, and we were often seeing significant calcium deposits in the coronary arteries of patients with normal blood flow studies. This would prove so helpful that we would eventually publish papers on it, in order to share our results with cardiologists around the world.

Early in the evolution of coronary artery disease, cholesterol deposits form in the walls of arteries, inducing the body to produce an inflammatory response. Over time, the cholesterol calcifies and becomes atherosclerotic plaque. Coronary calcium is an early marker of atherosclerotic plaque: the more calcium buildup, the more plaque. In other words, blockages can be present in patients with normal studies, but are not yet severe enough to affect the heart tracer's uptake into the heart muscle during stress. As we learned over time, calcium would also prove to be an independent predictor of future heart attacks and death. Because of the relationship between calcium and plaque, we began reporting what we realized was valuable prognostic information about calcium buildup in the coronary arteries to the treating physicians, who were responsible for starting therapy in the early phase of disease before the patients had heart attacks. We were excited about the change in our protocol, which we hoped would enable physicians to identify and treat atherosclerotic heart disease much earlier than before.

Coronary calcification is traditionally quantified via an Agatston score, a computer-generated measure of the total area and density of the calcium deposits in the arteries. Until we could get the funding to buy the software package that could perform Agatston scoring, we used a visual scoring system called the Shemesh Score. This test uses a subjective visual assessment of the extent of calcification in the four major coronary arteries, each of which is assigned a score from zero (no calcium) to three (calcium in greater than two-thirds of the entire length of that coronary artery), with a possible maximum score of twelve for the entire heart. However, the Shemesh system had never been used to read coronary calcium buildup on attenuation correction CT scans. Along with my cardiology colleague Dave Tang, I began using this visual scoring system on the attenuation correction scans to measure the amount of calcium buildup and determine its location in the coronary arteries. Given the test's subjective nature, Dave and I weren't sure that the respective calcium scores we gave would be the same, so we decided to do a study comparing the visual scores of the same patient produced by our two independent readings. In other words, we needed to validate that my visual coronary calcium score of four would equal Dave's visual coronary calcium score of four. We demonstrated excellent inter-reader reliability in a study of 150 patients, proving the reliability and reproducibility of our visual scoring technique, as well as the fact that this technique can be used to detect coronary artery disease in patients with normal blood flow. We presented our findings at a branch meeting of the Australian and New Zealand Society of Nuclear Medicine in Christchurch, where we won the Paul Orr Memorial Award for research, as well as at many other conferences in Australia and New Zealand.

Dr. Vitola and Dr. Better in Vienna

Finally, after getting statistical help from Massey University in Palmerston North, Dave and I presented our paper at the International Congress of Nuclear Cardiology in Vienna, Austria. The presentation was a great success, and one night over dinner in Vienna, a group of cardiologists led by Nathan Better and a Brazilian doctor named João Vitola drew up a proposal on a napkin for a multi-center international study. The study would look at how knowledge of coronary calcium scores would influence treating doctors to prescribe cholesterol-lowering medication. It was the birth of a study called the "Impact of Coronary Calcium Score as an Addition to Myocardial Perfusion Imaging in Altering Clinical Management," which we call called the ICCAMPA trial. My research in coronary calcium scoring would eventually become a major part of my professional life. This study and all the ancillary work that I and others in the cardiology field did regarding the importance of paying attention to coronary calcification was critical because it would give treating doctors a chance to intervene much earlier in the life of a patient with impending coronary problems, potentially staving off severe illness. More than anything else we did in our respective careers, it was on this occasion that we had the largest impact on the lives of many others at once. Instead of treating one individual patient with cholesterol blockages, we were providing information that would allow thousands of patients to receive better care.

Upon returning to New Zealand after the conference in Vienna, Dave and I noticed that our patients with calcium scores of zero on visual assessment—in other words, who had no calcium buildup in their coronary arteries—avoided having a subsequent heart attack or hospitalization with chest pain at six months. We presented these findings at the Cardiac Society of Australia and New Zealand's meeting in Perth, contending that a lack of calcification seemed to predict excellent heart health later on, including a lack of significant cholesterol buildup. A recent publication from the Netherlands also showed in such patients, there may be no additional benefit in doing expensive tests such as a myocardial perfusion scan. A calcium score of zero meant that patients were at low risk for obstructive coronary artery disease and had a long-term favorable outlook. In medicine, there are certain tests that are considered gatekeepers for determining whether further testing is warranted, and a calcium score of zero was proving to be ideal in this regard, particularly for patients over the age of fifty with stable chest pain. Since we had long wait times for heart scans at our clinic due to limited resources, we decided to prioritize those who were waiting according to their coronary calcium scores. If they had a score of zero, we could downgrade patients to very low risk, with less than 1 percent chance of death at five years, and avoid further testing. Thirty percent of our patients proved to have a calcium score of zero and did not need to undergo a nuclear medicine heart scan, thus avoiding unnecessary radiation exposure and the expense of further testing. This resulted in a reduction of our wait list from 120 patients to twenty-five patients, and a decrease in wait times from six months to only one month. And it allowed us to treat patients who most urgently needed intervention more swiftly.

To achieve long-term credibility and publish our results, however, we needed to back them up with Agatston scoring, which required us to buy software and hardware upgrades for our camera. We enrolled in a workshop at Massey University to encourage innovation at the hospital, called "the cutting-edge accelerator," which the hospital also sponsored. The workshop met weekly and helped us develop a business plan that we called the "Power of Zero." At the end of the workshop, we presented to the hospital administrators a potential cost-savings, through the use of Agatston screening, of $1,652 NZ per patient in those who had a calcium score of zero, because they would not require a nuclear medicine heart scan, which involves the use of an expensive radioactive isotope. The administration soon granted us approval to purchase the upgrade to our camera. Once the Agatston coronary calcium score screening protocol was up and running, we changed procedures so that for low-risk patients we administered only one scan—a stress heart study—cutting the expenses for these patients in half. This also saved time and reduced their radiation exposure. Ultimately, our research led to more efficient and productive cardiac imaging at our hospital, and also allowed for earlier diagnosis of the cause of chest pain in our patients. We avoided unnecessary testing, lowered costs and radiation exposure, reduced wait times, and did a better job at identifying low-risk patients who could safely qualify for early discharge.

———

After wading through the immense amount of paperwork required to get through the hospital's investigational review board, including a report on the study's impact on Māori patients, the ICCAMPA trial, whose concept we had drawn up at dinner in Vienna, was approved to enroll patients. This study was going to look mainly at how the knowledge of coronary calcium scores would influence treating doctors to prescribe cholesterol-lowering medication. After the heart scan, we would call the treating physicians and give them the results of the myocardial perfusion scan. We would ask them how the information would change their management of the patient and record their response. We would then give them the results of the coronary calcium score and ask them again how that information would change their management of the patients. We found that the addition of coronary calcium scores to the heart scans yielded significant changes in management in nearly half of all patients undergoing tests for suspected coronary artery disease. This was particularly evident in patients who were positive for coronary calcium despite a normal blood flow scan; their physicians could then alter their therapy, prescribing cholesterol-lowering medication as an early intervention. Patients who were over fifty and whose coronary calcium scores were zero, on the other hand, could avoid further expensive diagnostic testing that would not contribute to better outcomes.

Only by moving to New Zealand and practicing in a culture that prioritized preventive medicine was I able to help make these discoveries. Rather than being focused solely on making money, the institution where I was employed prioritized saving lives and reducing the cost of healthcare. I doubt that I would have had the same support for research on cost-reducing preventive approaches had I remained in the United States, much less the time to do original research in the first place.

Indeed, our work and its underlying message would be resisted by the profit-driven, procedure-oriented American cardiology community, but our research was embraced fully at my hospital and other hospitals like it, by resource-conscious Kiwi cardiologists, as well as by doctors practicing in similar settings around the world. This was to the great benefit of our patients, some of whom spent less time in a hospital setting due to their low calcium scores, and some of whom got better preventive care more swiftly than previously would have been initiated.

Before we began this work together, my colleagues had nominated me for an honor that further reinforced my sense of the ethical standards underpinning the practice of medicine in New Zealand. In 1518, King Henry VIII founded the Royal College of Physicians in England. My colleague Dave Tang submitted an evaluation of my first year in practice in New Zealand to the Australasian branch of the Royal College so that I could be considered for qualification to join the group. I had an interview at North Shore Hospital in Auckland that was conducted by a pair of cardiology physicians from the Royal Australasian College of Physicians. They went over my CV, discussed my clinical and research experience, and sent the college their evaluation. When the assignment committee finished its review, I could apply for Fellowship in the College. Given my emerg-

At Royal College ceremony
with fellow American

ing sensitivity to the differences between American medicine and Kiwi practices, I took particular note of the fact that the founding charter decreed this college would "curb the audacity of those wicked men who shall profess medicine more for the sake of their avarice than from the assurance of any good conscience." On June 19th of 2014, wearing a cap and gown, I formally joined the Royal Australasian College of Physicians at a ceremony in Cairns, Australia, and committed myself to the principles of this five-hundred-year-old institution and its traditions.

Many of my colleagues in the United States believed they were practicing medicine in a way that put them at the forefront of global research, but given my new vantage point from the other side of the world, I was coming to believe that the corporatization of American medicine forced doctors in the US to prioritize enticing patients into ever-costlier forms of intervention and testing, even when of unproven benefit. Cardiologists who perform large numbers of stent procedures, for instance, bring the most money to the hospitals and become some of the wealthiest practitioners in the nation, giving them tremendous influence both inside the typical American hospital and in Washington, DC, especially when it comes to healthcare reimbursement policies. Yet what families and loved ones really need from doctors are proven preventive approaches, rather than invasive procedures that do not offer additional benefits. So I felt proud of my time in New Zealand and the work we did there, because I believed it confirmed that by reducing costs and preventing illness, we were actually practicing medicine in a more humane fashion.

Given the differences I had observed between the US and New Zealand, as well as my research into preventive care, I became increasingly curious to compare how hospitals functioned and how patient care differed from one country to another. I was somewhat shocked to learn that even though medicine costs a great deal more in the United States, patient outcomes are not commensurately better there, and in fact are often worse. The United States spends more on healthcare than any other developed nation: 16.8 percent of its gross domestic product in 2019. The developed country that spends the lowest portion of its GDP on healthcare happens to be New Zealand, which spent roughly 9 percent of its GDP on healthcare in 2019. Health spending per person in the US was $11,945 in 2020, over $4,000 more than other high-income nations. Yet according to the United Nations Department of Economic and Social Affairs, the United States ranks forty-first among developed countries in the quality of its healthcare system, because it is neither effective nor efficient, while New Zealand's people-centered care ranks fourth. The United States is also the most obese nation in the world, and despite having the highest healthcare costs, it ranks forty-seventh in total population life expectancy at birth among developed nations, while New Zealand ranks twenty-second. You will live longer as a Kiwi, and it will cost both you and the country less. How can this be true? It defies common sense—until you realize that half the game is staying healthy in the first place and avoiding the dreadful expense and stress of serious illness. That's what I learned how to facilitate while practicing with my colleagues in New Zealand: we helped patients avoid the worst kinds of outcomes in the first place, instead of simply managing chronic heart disease by administering more and more interventions at astronomical costs.

That said, healthcare in New Zealand, while universally accessible, is sometimes challenged by limited resources. Some patients did not mind waiting for care, but when a patient needed care and felt an urgent desire to move forward, of course this could produce enormous stress. This was especially true when trying to get a patient accepted for valve replacement surgery or coronary bypass surgery at Wellington Hospital, our referral center. Wellington had a limited number of ICU beds, and when these were full, no one could be accepted for heart surgery. As the head nurse at Wellington ICU once said to me, it's a real dog's breakfast—in other words, it could be a mess at times, making do with the equivalent of table scraps. We would have a patient accepted for surgery, and while the patient was traveling in the ambulance to Wellington, the hospital would have an emergency admission to the ICU that would take that patient's post-op bed. Then our patient's surgery would be cancelled, and the ambulance would turn around and head back to our hospital. We sometimes had patients who had to wait weeks for heart surgery. They had to stay in our hospital the whole time, or else they would lose their place on the wait list.

I remember one bright executive in his forties who had a critical blockage of the left main coronary artery. He had presented with chest pain, and it soon became evident that he had a Type-A personality. He didn't take the waiting well. On morning rounds, I would find him sitting on the bed, his shoulder muscles taut, his jaw tightly closed, and the veins bulging near his piercing blue eyes. He finally was accepted for surgery, but while he was on the way down to Wellington, the hospital admitted an emergency case. Our patient's surgery was cancelled, and he was returned to our hospital. He became so distraught that he developed a bleeding gastric ulcer, which was very dangerous because he was on blood thinners to prevent clotting in his compromised coronary artery.

We stopped the blood thinners, he ceased bleeding, and eventually he received the necessary heart surgery, but the emotional upset he experienced from waiting that long almost cost him his life. We were so focused on treating his physical health problem that we let his mental health worsen his overall condition, teaching us once again that spirituality is an important part of the journey to wellness. But it was also a lesson in how limited resources and long wait times can have a significant impact on patient care. Would it have been better if we could have taken a more holistic approach and assisted that patient in learning how to curb his bodily responses to stress, and the effect on his mind and overall well-being? I think so, but even in New Zealand, medicine had not yet advanced to the point where that level of holistic care was available to him.

Chapter Nine

A TREMOR AND A FAREWELL

In 2018, when I was sixty-six years old, a slight tremor started manifesting when my right hand would get fatigued. The tremor would last about a minute, and I first noticed it while writing a procedure note in a patient's chart right after finishing an echocardiogram, during which I had been turning the transesophageal probe back and forth. I didn't think much of it at the time, but then I noticed another small tremor in the same hand when I was walking to the hospital one morning. There was no reason for my hand muscles to be tired at that hour, and I found the experience puzzling. The tremor resolved, and I did not notice it again for the rest of the day.

As a doctor, I knew that a tremor could occur for many different reasons, some of which might require attention, so I mentioned it to my general practitioner back in the United States. He swiftly referred me to a neurologist who, after taking a brief history, declared it was an "essential tremor," or a relatively benign condition that had no cure but typically did not progress. She assured me that I had nothing to worry about.

I did worry, though, because my mother's father had suffered through Parkinson's disease. I had vivid memories of him shuffling into the room back when I was growing up in California, during my Little League days. This was not Cecil, my paternal grandfather, upon whom I had relied so much for emotional support, but my maternal grandfather. Once upon a time, he too had been a jovial presence in my life. When I was even younger, I had known this grandfather to be an animated man with a happy-go-lucky personality. He had enjoyed telling us jokes and entertaining us—sometimes he would sing to us while playing two spoons, holding them so that their concave sides faced each other and tapping them on his knee to make a percussive sound. Like most grandfathers, he had wanted to make sure we had a good time in his company. Seeing him shut down had frightened me. I distinctly recall that he had what I would later learn is referred to as a "pill-rolling tremor," meaning a trembling of the fingers that makes it seem as though the person is rolling a pill between index finger and thumb. I could not help but wonder if the tremor that I was now experiencing might be an early sign of the same disease that had turned my maternal grandfather into a sad shadow of his formerly jovial self.

I went to a second neurologist, who performed a more detailed exam; he, too, reassured me that what I was experiencing was indeed an essential tremor and prescribed a beta blocker. Then I began to notice an occasional delay in my verbal interaction with people, as if someone had hit the pause button before I could summon my response to a question. I met with the chief of medical staff at our hospital, whose opinion I respected and trusted, and expressed my concern that the tremor might affect my performance as a clinical cardiologist, especially in the cath lab, where I was responsible for procedures during which one may not tremble at all without the possibility of dire consequences. He was very kind and suggested I see the hospital's staff physician, who reassured me that he saw no reason for concern and said that we should just keep an eye on my symptoms. I was supposed to let him know if they got worse.

Nothing ever took place while I was with a patient that compromised their care, yet I remained watchful of my own physical condition. I wondered if the assurances I had been given might prove false, and tried to be both patient and doctor to myself at the same time. I did not know whether to believe what I had been told and hope for the best, or to trust my own intuition that something was profoundly wrong. In discussing my symptoms one day with one of my internal medicine colleagues, I mentioned that I had begun having dreams where I would yell, punch, kick, and even leap out of bed. Once I had woken up on the floor. He told me that this was indicative of REM sleep behavior disorder, in which a person acts out their dreams. He added that most people with this disorder go on to develop Parkinson's. In other words, my physical response to dreaming was a lot like calcium deposits in my own patients' arteries: a harbinger of difficulty down the road. This doctor gave me a prescription for carbidopa-levodopa to see if it would help my tremor.

At the time, my tremor was so intermittent and mild that I couldn't tell if the medication made a difference, but I was becoming convinced that I had an early form of Parkinson's. I felt compelled to end my career before my condition could adversely affect somebody else's health. At this point in my life, my kids were starting to get married, and my mother's health was failing back in the United States. Also, Bonny wanted to return to Florida, to be closer to our family. With the unconfirmed suspicion that I probably had a progressive neurological disorder, I started to plan my retirement from my cardiology practice in New Zealand. I finished enrolling the fiftieth patient in our ICCAMPA study, wrote up our sites' results, and traveled to Melbourne with Bonny to hand over the original data forms to Nathan Better. I gave the hospital six months' notice to allow the administration ample time to recruit my replacement.

Once I had a patient who told me it is not how you start a relationship that tests your true character, but rather how you bring it to an end. Certainly this felt true to me at the time, as I had to summon up every ounce of courage I possessed to make a graceful exit under these trying circumstances. I wanted to give back to the country that had given so much to me, and arranged to donate one hundred thousand New Zealand dollars to the hospital's medical trust to support education and research in coronary calcium, the most important legacy of my own time as a physician in New Zealand. In 2019, at the age of sixty-eight, I formally retired. I tried to hide from everybody how devastating all of this was for me emotionally, because I had loved being a doctor, and did not really want to stop working. Furthermore, I felt fearful of my own future, having witnessed my grandfather's alteration from a lively and warm presence into a frozen figure, a person who had great difficulty both speaking and walking. Toward the end, he even had a hard time mustering up a smile, as the Parkinson's changed his face from a fluid countenance into an immobile mask. Like so many physicians and nurses, I knew all too well the course of my own likely demise.

My colleagues could nonetheless see everything that I was going through, and they gathered around me in all sorts of ways. I was grateful to have a farewell *pōwhiri* ceremony to honor my time in New Zealand. Our Māori cardiology clinic nurse, Carol, who had always supported me through difficult times, organized the *pōwhiri* at one of my patients' *marae* in Rangimarie, a sacred site where a tribe holds traditional events in a longhouse designed to accommodate weddings, funerals, and important meetings. This also happened to be the *marae* of Sir Mason Durie, the Māori psychiatrist who had related the story of the young girl who had been hallucinating due to a virus.

After friendly intentions had been established, our hosts called us into the *marae*. The woman caller standing at the porch began a chant to summon the visitors into the longhouse. In the first part of the ceremony, while we were still near the gated entrance of the property, our Māori hosts welcomed us, and we responded by thanking them and acknowledging the ancestors who came before. We then began moving slowly forward until we reached the porch of the longhouse where the caller stood. Inside the longhouse, where paintings of their ancestors lined the walls, our hosts began a more formal welcome of the *manuhiri*, or visitors, by the *tangata whenua*, the people of the land or home people. The Māori lead male, or chief, who was the husband of one of my patients, performed this part of the ceremony. He acknowledged the support and love of the ancestors. He acknowledged the sacred mountains, rivers, and lakes that make up this region of New Zealand, which I had visited and felt sad to be leaving behind, maybe forever. After everyone sang a song, I stood up to speak, and I welcomed everyone in Māori, saying *"Tena koutou katoa,"* as Carol had taught me. I then spoke about my experiences in New Zealand, and some of my Māori patients related their impression of me as a doctor. They said they were grateful as I had treated them and that their conditions had improved.

After the ceremony, we returned to the dining hall for a lunch that the people of the *marae* had prepared. I could feel their warm embrace and it left me comforted, honored, and happy.

I had another farewell ceremony at Zest, the café across the street from the hospital. Here, I presented the check to the medical trust and expressed my gratitude to all those who had worked with me to research the calcium scoring effort. Afterwards, I was surprised when my colleagues in the cardiology department gave me a green stone *pounamu* necklace, which each person held in their hands in order to pass their spirit, or *wairua*, into the stone for me to carry back to Florida. The *pounamu* has great spiritual gravitas and is given on significant occasions of "honor, respect, and permanence." The stones are passed down from generation to generation and serve as a spiritual investment to retain the positive influences they bring to the wearer. I felt blessed and honored by the recognition of the six-and-a-half years I had spent in New Zealand. It felt as though my colleagues were saying they had accepted me into their family, and I was now one of their own. And then it was time to say goodbye.

Last day in cath lab

Chapter Ten

BACK HOME

After Bonny and I returned to the United States, I scheduled an appointment with a neurologist at the clinic who was an expert in Parkinson's disease. He was confident that I did indeed have Parkinson's, and he also prescribed Carbidopa-Levodopa for the tremor. In his own research, he had discovered one of the genes that is involved in the development of the disease; I was tested for the gene but ended up not having it. Still, the doctor was certain I would manifest further symptoms. The question of whether or not I would go on to develop Parkinson's no longer remained a mystery, but rather a dark cloud on the horizon portending eventual rain. Alas, I had been right all along, when I had never so badly wanted to be proven wrong. Thankfully I continue to do well to this day, playing golf as often as possible and staying upright and steady on my feet out on the green, on continual medical treatment and with little progression of symptoms.

Exercise became paramount, and I began seeing a trainer two to three times a week. With age-related Parkinson's, the end game is all about staving off decline, and I was willing to try anything, including micro-dosing of psilocybin. That helped my mood, if not my physical condition, and the pervasive sadness I had been grappling with began to dissipate. Eventually, I even came to feel lucky that all I had was a tremor and a notable slowness to my speech. With more hours to spend on recreational pursuits, I arranged to spend as much time as possible with members of my family, played golf every day, kept up my reading on coronary calcium, and continued my medical education in other arenas as well. My son and I began attending national football league games in Jacksonville, Florida, to see the Jaguars play during their home games. We went every Sunday that we could get to the stadium. Bonny and I had held onto our home in Jacksonville the whole time we were gone, and a couple from Bosnia had moved into the upstairs portion. They remained in the rooms our children had once occupied, and we began sharing our residence with them and their six-year-old, Ella. After our son bought a house nearby and began renovating that property with his partner, our dinner table grew crowded in the evenings, bringing both Bonny and I a lot of joy. Life was good. Or, as they say in New Zealand, good as gold.

Shortly after I returned home, however, I began to grapple with an even more dire medical situation: my mother's precarious health. My mother was a frail ninety-five-year-old with renal insufficiency who had developed recurrent deep vein thrombosis, or blood clots in the veins of her legs, and she was started on what doctors like to call first-line therapy with an oral blood thinner. For some reason, the aspirin she had been prescribed previously was not discontinued, and taking both medications at once caused her to develop a gastrointestinal bleed after about a week.

She was hospitalized, both the blood thinner and aspirin were discontinued, and she received an emergency blood transfusion.

I was in Chicago, Illinois at the time, at a men's golf outing with friends, and I was at dinner with that group when my younger brother called to tell me that our mother was in the hospital. I immediately prepared to fly home to Jacksonville, and from there to Charlottesville, Virginia, to be present as her care continued. Before I could arrive in Virginia, however, my mother underwent an upper endoscopy which was negative except for a small hiatal hernia. My sister was with our mother at the time, and she put our mother's gastroenterologist on the phone with me. He explained that there was no evidence of a bleeding ulcer, and all they had found was the hernia, which I knew about already from her past care. But they had also performed an abdominal CT, and the gastroenterologist informed us that she appeared to have a mass in her colon. He told me he did not recommend a colonoscopy, as it could be too much for a ninety-five-year-old to bear. I respected his restraint and caution, given my mother's age and fragile condition. My mother's bleeding soon stopped, and her blood count stabilized. After an ultrasound showed clots still present in the deep veins of the legs, however, the hospitalist scheduled her to undergo an invasive procedure called an inferior vena cava filter, to prevent a blood clot traveling to the lung.

I spoke with my sister, and we communicated to the hospitalist that before we agreed to the filter, we wanted to talk more about the wisdom of doing an invasive procedure like that on a ninety-five-year-old with renal insufficiency. We were concerned about the venogram that would be done for placement of the filter, during which dye is injected into the vena cava to identify where the blood supply to the kidneys arrives, as the filter needs to be placed below the blood supply to the kidneys. I had injected dye into patients every day as a cardiologist, so I was aware of the adverse effects that dye can have on elderly patients; I had seen dye knock out their kidneys more than once.

We were told the interventional radiologist who normally did the filter placement procedure was out of town and unable to speak with us, but that he would be back on the morning the procedure was to be performed. Then I learned that, while I was on my way to Virginia, my brother had been unable to get help from the nursing staff to take our mother to the bathroom, and that our mother had also not been given any breakfast. When my siblings subsequently asked why she hadn't received a meal, they were told that it was to keep her stomach empty prior to the inferior vena cava filter procedure. In other words, the hospital was planning to move forward with the procedure that we had asked them not to do without discussing it with us. My sister quickly called the hospitalist and cancelled the procedure.

I landed at the airport in Charlottesville, where my brother picked me up. My mother had already gone home on a lower dose of the blood thinner Eliquis, and without the aspirin. When I got to her house, she looked remarkably well, just a little bit weak. "I love you," she said to me, as soon as I got there. I loved her too, which was why I felt upset and disappointed by her treatment at the hospital. Inferior vena cava filter procedures bring in thousands of dollars to hospitals, but for the majority of patients, they have no proven benefit over medical therapy with blood thinners for deep vein thrombosis in preventing blood clots to the lung. While inferior vena cava filters do have an important role in preventing blood clots from traveling to the lung in patients with histories of pulmonary embolism, they are also associated with multiple complications, and do nothing to address the painful leg swelling associated with the clots. Furthermore, the interventional radiologist who was going to do the procedure had not discussed any of this with our family, even though my mother was clearly a fragile patient. From our family's perspective, the hospital staff had been too busy to empty a bed pan, but seemed ready to administer an expensive and invasive procedure without a careful discussion of the risks.

Unfortunately, my mother, God bless her, was eventually diagnosed with terminal colon cancer. I believed that the doctor who had scheduled the expensive intervention either knew or should have known this at the time, given her abnormal abdominal CT, but had scheduled the procedure anyway. In other words, this doctor had failed to treat her holistically as a patient. To me, it seemed clear that there was no reason to intervene at the risk of causing additional suffering, given the colon cancer. They simply needed to let go of the imperative to act, and to make her as comfortable as possible, since her condition was terminal—to let her find the easiest way to exit this life and in her own time "suck the kumara," as my Kiwi colleagues would have said. At home with us, she continued to lose weight and strength, and she passed away peacefully under hospice care in the middle of the night about a month later. That is as close to a good ending as any of us get, in my opinion, and I have witnessed the ending of many lives. It brought me and my siblings great peace of mind to know we averted unnecessary suffering in her final hours and brought her home, where she felt most at ease. Her ashes will be buried alongside the graves of my grandfather, my grandmother, and my father, on a hill overlooking the farm in the Shenandoah Valley. That is where my sister now lives, and where my brothers have a property just down the road. Grief visits us all anyway, in its own unique form, no matter how well cared for a loved one may be in their final hours. I found that I went numb, while my sister cried every time I tried to speak about our mother, and my brothers withdrew, shaken. They are barely ready to talk about the celebration of life that we hope to plan together, while I am perhaps too ready to talk about it in the dispassionate way that we doctors are taught to adopt as we respond to the vagaries of everybody else's lives.

After my mother died, I took respite in work once again. I learned the paper I had written and rewritten with colleagues about our work on coronary calcium would finally be published. The paper had gone through about ten revisions, as editors had requested various clarifications, and I had almost given up hope that it would ever appear in a journal. Then it found a home in the *Journal of Nuclear Cardiology*, the preeminent journal read by those in my profession, appearing online just days after my mother passed away. I found its publication bolstering, something solid I could hold onto as the winds of change howled by. Now the entire field of cardiology has full access to the work that we did. It has also been exciting to learn that the American Society of Nuclear Cardiology now recommends that all myocardial perfusion studies should be done with chest CT and a reading of coronary calcium, as we did in our study. We helped establish a new standard of care in nuclear cardiology. My fervent hope, before I die myself, is to witness a sea change in how medicine is practiced, with a greater focus on disease prevention across the board. More and more people are being diagnosed before becoming symptomatic, and it's during those early phases that there is a real opportunity to make a difference.

When we left New Zealand, I brought home not only my little red book filled with Kiwi slang, but also a respect for the underlying philosophy that spiritual health is an important part of the journey to physical health. That is what I learned in New Zealand, practicing with finite resources alongside so many other hopeful men and women: to remain cheerful and steadfast in the face of life's challenges, and to walk toward any unavoidable difficulty with the assurance of good conscience and a chin held high. Halfway around the world, I found confirmation that while practicing medicine, one can proceed in perpetual search of what is right, holding the question before oneself like a beacon to illuminate the way. On reflection, perhaps that was what my grandfather had been instructing me to do, with his stories about my great-grandfather. Thus we can hold in our minds that guiding principle—always aim to be a true humanitarian—and follow the path lit up before us.

Afterword

by Kirsten Stowers Bos

When I was young, I did not fully comprehend what my dad did for a living, but I always felt a sense of pride every time I told my classmates that he was a heart doctor. I switched to the term heart doctor from cardiologist because my fellow kindergartners didn't quite grasp what a cardiologist was yet, and quite frankly neither did I. My entire life, strangers would come up to me and say, "Your dad saved my life." Even our next-door neighbor reminded me of what he owed my father every time we'd see him in passing. I knew that my dad was heroic and that his job was all-encompassing. His responsibilities to his patients meant that he was on call many evenings and weekends and would have to leave in the middle of dinner or on a Sunday afternoon while we were at the beach. He often couldn't make it to dance recitals, sports games, or school events, and our family missed him. But it all seemed to be okay because, after all, he was saving lives.

I got a much better understanding of what my dad did when I was nine years old and had the opportunity to shadow him at work. My memory of that day is like a movie filmed in one continuous shot, following the protagonist through a whirlwind of activity. First, we left his private practice and took the seemingly long walk over to the hospital. Along the way, we greeted Dad's colleagues, and it seemed like he knew everyone. We passed the vending machines, cafeteria, and gift shop until finally we walked through the swinging doors of the private employee entrance. Then we were inside the hospital. It was an otherworldly environment full of beeping noises and people rushing in every direction. Later we entered an operating room. My dad's coworkers lit up when they saw him. They told me how my dad loved to play the song "Smooth Operator" by Sade every time he operated. I knew my dad to have only two CDs in his car my entire life, music by Sade and by Enya, so things were starting to add up.

Then we moved into a patient care room, where a woman was lying in a hospital bed. She jumped up from the bed as soon as she saw my dad, gave him a big hug and kiss, and told him she loved him. I had never met or even heard of this woman in my life, so being the inquisitive kid I was, I asked, "Who the heck are you?" She began to tell me in a thick Brooklyn accent that my dad had saved her life and how if she were half her age my mom would have something to worry about. Half-terrified and half-impressed, I spoke with her more and began to see the effect my dad had on other people's lives. This was something he rarely described to us, so seeing it firsthand had a huge impact on me. At Christmas time, our home would fill with spring rolls from one patient, oranges from another, as well as candies, bottles of wine, and the like from the many people my dad had cared for over the years. This book goes into many of my dad's experiences in the medical field. I am proud of his vulnerability and the courage that it took for him to write this book. I'm sure the stories that he shared made you laugh and cry, but I hope they also leave you feeling galvanized about seeking change in our healthcare system.

KIWI SLANG

(Little Red Book, complete version)

Ambo: Ambulance

Aye: what, or a syllable used at the end of a sentence to signal agreement

Banger: sausage

Batch: holiday home

Biro: pen

Bolshy: uncooperative, deliberately difficult

Bonnet: car hood

Boot: car trunk

Box of birds: happy, joyful, feeling good

Boy racer: driving a fast car

Box of fluffy ducks: especially happy, joyful

Blowing a Hooley: strong wind

Brassed off: annoyed

Brekkie: breakfast

Bro: friend

Brolly: umbrella

Bugger off: piss off

Bum: butt

Choice: good

Carked it: died

Chuffed: pleased, happy

Chur: thanks; cool, sweet

Couldn't organize a piss-up in a brewery: very bad at organizing

Crickey Dick: holy s***; wow

Crook: sick

Crumbly: old, frail

Cuppa: hot cup of tea or coffee

Cuz/cuzzy: friend

Chips: fries

Crisps: chips

Dag: hard case joker

Dairy: convenience store

Ditch: the Tasman Sea between New Zealand and Australia

Dog's breakfast: a complete mess; an unappealing mixture of table scraps

Doing the ton: speeding (ton = 100 kilometers/hour)

Dunny: toilet

Fagged: worn out

Fortnight: two weeks

Fringe: bangs

Fanny: female genitalia

Feed: a meal

Fill your boots: get as much as you can

Fizzy: soda pop

Flash: really good-looking

Gap it: leave, take off

Ga day: good day (hello)

Gob smacked: shocked

Good as gold: good job; not a problem

Good on ya: well done

Go to custard/turn to custard: plans that don't work out

Grotty: unpleasant, in poor condition

Haka: Māori chant performed by men

Hangi: Māori traditional cuisine cooked on hot rocks

Heaps: a lot

Happy as Larry: very happy

Huckery: poor quality, shabby, ugly

Jandals: sandals, flip flops

Judder bar: speed bump

Kia Ora: hi; good luck; be well (Māori)

Kiwi: New Zealander

Knackered: worn out, tired

Lolly: candy

L&P: Lemon & Paeroa, a brand of lemon-flavored soda water

Manky: worthless, inferior, dirty, unpleasant

Mana: great character and prestige

Matey Patatey: real good friend

Mint: cool or awesome

Murder a brown snake: have a bowel movement (Aussie slang)

Nappy: diaper

Nana: grandma

Netball: basketball without the dribble

Niggle: irritation

OTP: on the piss (drinking)

Oz: Australia

Pākehā: white New Zealander

Piss: beer

Pissed: drunk

Piss off: go away

(take the) Piss out of: to joke or kid

Piss-up: drinking party

POME: Prisoner of Mother England (slang for someone from England)

Pop my clogs: to die

Porkie pies: lies

Pōwhiri: Māori welcome ceremony

Pram: baby carriage

Prang: motor vehicle accident

Pulling a swifty: pulling a fast one, deceiving someone

Pull a sickie: take a mental health day

Puffed: short of breath

Puffing like Billyoh: very short of breath

Rattle your dags: hurry up

Reckon: to believe

Right said, Fred: OK; well said

Rooted: feeling tired, knackered

Root: to have sex

Rug up: bundle up

Serviette: napkin

Shagged: tired; to have sexual intercourse

Shag pile: private office

She'll be right: it will be OK; no worries

She's jake: it's OK; good

Shonky: no good, dodgy

Shoot the gap: leave, to go

Shout: buying a round of drinks or a meal

Skiting: showing off

Skive off: avoid going to work or school

Skux: stud, ladies' man; beyond awesome

Sparrow's fart: very early in the morning

Spit the dummy: throw a tantrum

Sprog: a child

Spunk: good looks

Stroppy: agitated, easily provoked

Stuffed up: to have made a mistake

Sunnies: sunglasses

Suck the kumara: to die

Suss: to take care of a task that needs sorting out

Sweet-as: cool, awesome

Take-away: take-out

Tea: dinner

Tell a porkie: tell a lie

Tight as: stingy

Toey: nervous

Togs: swimsuit

Tramping: hiking

Torch: flashlight

Twig: did not realize

Wag off/wagging: skip work, school

Wellies: gumboots

Wop-wops: wilderness

Wee bit: little bit

Wee cracker of a day: great day

Went down for a 6: fell down; hit a home run (cricket)

Wee yarn: a little chat

Yarn: chat

Yonks: longtime, forever

Zed: Z

Acknowledgments

Writing about my life has been a bit one-sided. I've told almost all of the good and glossed over a bit of the bad. While trying to put a positive spin on my life and my profession in order to inspire young people to go into medicine, I have left out some of the unfortunate experiences, such as the patient in New Zealand who had a complication from a catheterization that I did. The patient bled from the puncture wound, had to go to surgery, suffered a complicated course, and ended up dying. That is extremely unusual, and it haunts me still. I will acknowledge that here, but mostly I want to give thanks.

My accomplishments would not have been possible without the cooperation of many talented people whom I would like to name:

My editor and cheerleader, Helen Thorpe.

My wife and cheerleader, Bonny, as well as our entire family, especially our children Lauren, Christian, Kirsten, and Jeffery.

My colleagues Amen Sergew, Nathan Better, João Vitola, Darri Karlsson, Dave Tang, Adrian Lamballe, Buster Browning, and Michael Koren.

My initial editor, Jerry Nelson.

My niece, Kerry Wekelo.

My nuclear medicine tech in Florida, Nancy DeLoach.

Our friends in New Zealand, all of them, and our inner circle there: Reena and John Wallace, Sue Blewitt, Arunee and Keng Srichantra, as well as the Afghan families whom we had the privilege to serve and learn from along the way.

The nurses I have worked with throughout my career—people I like to call "the soul of medicine"—have been amazing human beings. In New Zealand, the hospital nurses I worked with and want to thank by first name are: Richard, Lia, Dean, Lijoy, Amy, Stephanie, Carol, Claire, and Erin. I would also like to thank our cardiology tech Jasmine Sobith, our nuclear medicine tech Clare McKenzie, our pharmacist Anthea Gregan, and our chief medical officer, Ken Clark.

Without everyone listed above, my career and this book would not have been possible. Thanks to one and all.

Bibliography

Al-Mallah, Mouaz H., Timothy M. Bateman, Kelley R. Branch, Andrew Crean, Eric L. Gingold, Randall C. Thompson, Sarah E. McKenney, et al. "2022 ASNC/AAPM/SCCT/SNMMI Guideline for the Use of CT in Hybrid Nuclear/CT Cardiac Imaging." *Journal of Nuclear Cardiology* 29, no. 6 (September 2, 2022): 3491–3535. https://doi.org/10.1007/s12350-022-03089-z.

Alexander, John H., and Peter K. Smith. "Coronary-Artery Bypass Grafting." *New England Journal of Medicine* 375, no. 10 (September 8, 2016). https://doi.org/10.1056/nejmc1608042.

Bismark, Marie, and Ron Paterson. "No-Fault Compensation in New Zealand: Harmonizing Injury Compensation, Provider Accountability, and Patient Safety." *Health Affairs* 25, no. 1 (2006): 278–83. https://doi.org/10.1377/hlthaff.25.1.278.

Boden, William E., Robert A. O'Rourke, Koon K. Teo, Pamela M. Hartigan, David J. Maron, William J. Kostuk, Merril Knudtson, et al. "Optimal Medical Therapy with or without PCI for Stable Coronary Disease." *New England Journal of Medicine* 356, no. 15 (April 12, 2007): 1503–16. https://doi.org/10.1056/nejmoa070829.

Engbers, Elsemiek M., Jorik R. Timmer, Jan Paul Ottervanger, Mohamed Mouden, Siert Knollema, and Pieter L. Jager. "Prognostic Value of Coronary Artery Calcium Scoring in Addition to Single-Photon Emission Computed Tomographic Myocardial Perfusion Imaging in Symptomatic Patients." *Circulation: Cardiovascular Imaging* 9, no. 5 (May 10, 2016). https://doi.org/10.1161/circimaging.115.003966.

Evans, Melanie, Max Rust, and Tom McGinty. "Big Nonprofit Hospitals Expand in Wealthier Areas, Shun Poorer Ones." The Wall Street Journal. Dow Jones & Company, December 26, 2022. https://www.wsj.com/articles/nonprofit-hospitals-deals-tax-breaks-11672068264.

Jayadeva, Pavithra S., Stephen Stowers, E. W. Tang, João Vitola, Rodrigo Cerci, Jessica Yao, James Westcott, Barry Elison, and Nathan Better. "The Impact of Coronary Calcium Score as an Addition to Myocardial Perfusion Imaging in Altering Clinical Management (ICCAMPA Trial)." *Journal of Nuclear Cardiology*, September 12, 2022. https://doi.org/10.1007/s12350-022-03086-2.

Khera, Amit V., Connor A. Emdin, Isabel Drake, Pradeep Natarajan, Alexander G. Bick, Nancy R. Cook, Daniel I. Chasman, et al. "Genetic Risk, Adherence to a Healthy Lifestyle, and Coronary Disease." *New England Journal of Medicine* 375, no. 24 (December 15, 2016): 2349–58. https://doi.org/10.1056/nejmoa1605086.

Maron, David J., Judith S. Hochman, Harmony R. Reynolds, Sripal Bangalore, Sean M. O'Brien, William E. Boden, Bernard R. Chaitman, et al. "Initial Invasive or Conservative Strategy for Stable Coronary Disease." *New England Journal of Medicine* 382, no. 15 (April 9, 2020): 1395–1407. https://doi.org/10.1056/nejmoa1915922.

Mehta, Laxmi S., Sandra J. Lewis, Claire S. Duvernoy, Anne K. Rzeszut, Mary Norine Walsh, Robert A. Harrington, Athena Poppas, Mark Linzer, Philip F. Binkley, and Pamela S. Douglas. "Burnout and Career Satisfaction among U.S. Cardiologists." *Journal of the American College of Cardiology* 73, no. 25 (July 2, 2019): 3345–48. https://doi.org/10.1016/j.jacc.2019.04.031.

Michos, Erin D., John W. McEvoy, and Roger S. Blumenthal. "Lipid Management for the Prevention of Atherosclerotic Cardiovascular Disease." *New England Journal of Medicine* 381, no. 16 (October 17, 2019): 1557–67. https://doi.org/10.1056/nejmra1806939.

Nasir, Khurram, Jagat Narula, and Martin B. Mortensen. "Message for Upcoming Chest Pain Management Guidelines." *Journal of the American College of Cardiology* 76, no. 21 (November 24, 2020): 2433–35. https://doi.org/10.1016/j.jacc.2020.09.593.

"New Zealand Cardiac Surgery National Report 2018." Ministry of Health NZ. New Zealand Government - Te Kāwanatanga o Aotearoa, November 5, 2020.

https://www.health.govt.nz/publication/new-zealand-cardiac-surgery-national-report-2018.

"New Zealand vs United States Health Stats Compared." NationMaster.com. NationMaster. Accessed February 12, 2023. https://www.nationmaster. com/country-info/compare/New-Zealand/United-States/Health.

O'Connor, Anahad. "Heart Stents Still Overused, Experts Say." The New York Times. The New York Times Company, August 15, 2013. https://archive.nytimes.com/well.blogs.nytimes.com/2013/08/15/ heart-stents-continue-to-be-overused/.

Ornish, Dean. *Dr. Dean Ornish's Program for Reversing Heart Disease*. New York, NY: Ballantine Bks, 1990.

"Overview of the Health System." Ministry of Health NZ. New Zealand Government - Te Kāwanatanga o Aotearoa, July 1, 2022. https://www.health. govt.nz/new-zealand-health-system/overview-health-system.

"Physician Practice Benchmark Survey." American Medical Association. American Medical Association, October 14, 2022. https://www.ama-assn. org/about/research/physician-practice-benchmark-survey.

"Quality of Care." World Health Organization. World Health Organization. Accessed February 12, 2023. https://www.who.int/health-topics/ quality-of-care#tab=tab_1.

Roberts, Catherine. "Why Hospitals Need to Share Heart Surgery Success Rates." Consumer Reports. Consumer Reports, April 6, 2017. https:// www.consumerreports.org/heart-surgery/why-hospitals-need-to-share-surgery-success-data/.

Rosenbaum, Lisa. "The Whole Ball Game — Overcoming the Blind Spots in Health Care Reform." *New England Journal of Medicine* 368, no. 10 (March 7, 2013): 959–62. https://doi.org/10.1056/nejmms1301576.

"Rural Hospital Closures Threaten Access: Solutions to Preserve Care in Local Communities." American Hospital Association. American Hospital Association, September 2022. https://www.aha.org/system/files/media/ file/2022/09/rural-hospital-closures-threaten-access-report.pdf.

Shanafelt, Tait D., Sonja Boone, Litjen Tan, Lotte N. Dyrbye, Wayne Sotile, Daniel Satele, Colin P. West, Jeff Sloan, and Michael R. Oreskovich. "Burnout and Satisfaction with Work-Life Balance among Us Physicians Relative to the

General US Population." *Archives of Internal Medicine* 172, no. 18 (October 8, 2012): 1377. https://doi.org/10.1001/archinternmed.2012.3199.

Stowers, Stephen A., Paul Gilmore, Mack Stirling, James M. Morantz, Alan B. Miller, Laura J. Meyer, Gary Glazer, and Douglas Behrendt. "Cardiac Pheochromocytoma Involving the Left Main Coronary Artery Presenting with Exertional Angina." *American Heart Journal* 114, no. 2 (August 1987): 423–27. https://doi.org/10.1016/0002-8703(87)90513-8.

Tikkanen, Roosa, and Melinda K. Abrams. "U.S. Health Care from a Global Perspective, 2019: Higher Spending, Worse Outcomes?" CommonwealthFund.org. The Commonwealth Fund, January 30, 2020. https://www.commonwealthfund.org/publications/issue-briefs/2020/jan/us-health-care-global-perspective-2019.

About the Author

Stephen Stowers is a skilled clinician who practiced cardiology for twenty-nine years in Florida and six and a half years on the North Island of New Zealand as a member of the Royal Australasian College of Physicians. Dr. Stowers graduated from the University of Virginia School of Medicine. He completed his cardiology fellowship at the George Washington University Hospital. As a pioneering cardiologist, he was a leader in the development of acute imaging of chest pain patients in the emergency room. Dr. Stowers has published widely in medical literature and recently published an international study on coronary calcium and its potential contribution to the early detection and treatment of coronary artery disease. He has also written a popular blog about his life in New Zealand, kiwicardiology.com. This is his first book.

www.ingramcontent.com/pod-product-compliance
Lightning Source LLC
Chambersburg PA
CBHW061345160726
47995CB00001B/185